Dedication

This book is dedicated to my mother, Anne Marie Spencer and her children Charles, Charlene and Debra. There were many hard times when we were young, you all worked multiple jobs and long hours allowing our family to survive and conquer our circumstances. Although our home often had no heat or food, we fed on motivation and warmed ourselves with caring and support of each other. I owe all my achievements to the strong family bond which was created through those nights we baked flour, sugar and cinnamon to eat and talked gathered in the kitchen to sleep near the oven for warmth. My love as always goes out to all of you.

Foundations of Network Technology 2.0
Table of Contents
Page I of II

Foundations of Network Technology 2.0
Table of Contents
Page II of II

Chapter 1
Introduction to the book

Introduction to the book:

There are a number of concepts in the field of network technology. In most developed countries, network technology exists in almost every part of our existence. Our cars have systems which interact with cell towers. Our homes have cameras which can be activated by smart phones. We order tickets for events via a website and doctors participate in group surgery between countries via streaming video. Our civilization has truly progressed to a technology-driven society. Due to the 1960's premonitions of what the future would include, I often hear people say, "Where is my flying car?!" When I hear that sentence, I smile to myself for I know the answer to that question. It is not that the flying car has not been created,..most people simply can't afford one so companies don't mass produce it.

The People Who need this book:

This book is structured in a format to allow motivated individuals to perform a number of high-order network technology tasks. Everyone whom purchases this book may not be interested in certification but simply desire to increase their knowledge in network technology. The subjects covered in this text are related to installation and maintenance of specific network technology such as Routers, Switches and Remote Access methods. The topics listed in this book are the foundation of every large network. Through the use of practical (Or what is referred to as "Hands-On") activities, the readers of this book will master the foundations of network technology and be able to perform all required tasks to implement the technology relying only on their accumulated knowledge developed through study, repetition and successful practice.

Introduction to Field of Network Technology:

For those whom purchased this book to increase their knowledge in order to attain a certification in network technology, congratulations! You have the correct book in hand! The tasks which are displayed in the text are directly related to a number of certifications offered by Cisco and Comptia. One of the excellent aspects of understanding one vendor of network technology is the ability to "Cross-Learn" other vendor technologies. The term "IP address" is used for servers, routers, printers and cell phones. These "network device" identities are used on all of the technologies mentioned above. The only difference is "where" you would insert the settings on each platform. This book is created in a "survey-course" fashion and was developed to give the reader the ability to firmly understand network technologies and to implement them in a production environment ("Real World"). The implementation is based upon "foundation understanding" and utilization of actual technology. Persons presently working full-time in the network technology field will benefit from the tasks in this text to learn the technology in order to enhance their organization's ability and functions. Persons who desire to enter the field of network technology will benefit from developing a practical understanding of what is required for network devices to communicate and offer support services on a network or the internet.

Importance of having Network Certifications:

There are a number of certifications available in the field of network technology. It is important that persons interested in the field understand the foundation of what each certification indicates in order to better position themselves in the job market. Many persons outside of the field have heard of different certifications. Certifications themselves do not make a person better at completing job tasks then someone who has no certifications. Certifications do have some essential truths to them which make their attainment highly desirable. It is regarded as true that a person who has certifications will possess the following qualities:

- **Greater knowledge of a specific technology than those without the Certification.**
  - Persons working in the field for many years primarily know tasks and technologies which they have been exposed to via job assignment or troubleshooting situations. The unfortunate association with the learning process is that the person has not been exposed to all of the primary features of a technology. Many features can save an organization money as opposed to purchasing many other devices which provide a function that the "on-site" technology already has built into it.

- **Display of letters for hiring entity (i.e., Human Resources, Selection Committee, etc.).**
  - Often times, the group responsible for the hiring process will not understand all the particulars surrounding the qualifications necessary to fill a technology position. In addition, after learning of all the requirements, it often becomes expensive to advertise all the desired criteria for an application to be successful in interview selection (Often times, job advertising companies charge the company looking for applicants based upon how many words are in the advertisement

(Often $1 per word, charged every week the advertisement is available in newspaper or internet format). To compensate for the "word length" of the job advertisement and the review of applications eligible for interview, hiring entities often ask their associates for a better way of advertising a position with the least amount of "words" as possible. This normally results in the hiring entity being told some technology "abbreviations" to use instead of descriptive paragraphs. Take the following scenario for example if the job announcement would cost $1 per month per word:

> **Option A**: Human Resources person creates job announcement (Total cost about $51 dollars per month):
   ❖ The technology department needs a person who can perform the following:
      1. Install Network Operating Systems.
      2. Install, configure and troubleshoot Hubs.
      3. Install, configure and troubleshoot Switches
      4. Troubleshoot network connections on computers.
      5. Address printer problems.
      6. Answer phones on the Help Desk.
      7. Connect and install Category 5 cable in building.
      8. Connect network devices on LAN.

> **Option B**: Human Resources person creates job announcement (Total cost about $8 dollars per month):
   ❖ The technology department needs an Net+ Certified technician.

o Human Resources will now look for applications with the appropriate letters. Other applicants might have years of experience working on network devices. Their resumes might also list every item on the job announcement. Human Resources often look at hundreds of resumes per day, however. In fact, some companies have "Optical Character Recognition" (Often called "OCR" software which reads over all the resumes as they arrive via e-mail or posted to a job website. Human Resources attempts to be as efficient as possible, so they will only respond to those resumes which have the "Certification Letters" they were anticipating.

Examples of International Network Technology Certifications:

There are a number of certifications which are international (Valid all over the world). The certifications of these types were created by large organizations and professionals in the field of network technology. Information combined from full-time professionals, educators, and technicians was combined to create the "The Handbook of Occupational Job Titles". This document is used to identify definite and specific tasks a "Network Technology" specialist would have to perform and have knowledge. Some certifications are "vendor neutral" (Used for multiple companies and technologies) while others are "proprietary" (Offered exclusively by a specific company or organization). In order to gain industry certification, it is often required that a person pass some number of examinations or assessments hosted by the organization which sponsors the specific certification. Your desired area specialty in network technology will define which certification might be the most advantageous for you to attain. Some certifications which were active at the time of writing this book are as follows:

- **Net+ (Network+)** = Offered by a worldwide organization known as "CompTIA (Computer Technicians International Association). The Net+ often viewed as a "survey" certification. The primary focus of the certification is "Concepts and Knowledge". The certification examination assesses multiple terms existing in network technology from the perspective of many different devices from multiple companies. The examination does not focus on any single technology or process from start to finish. This is often viewed as the "Entry Level" network technology certification.
- **CCT (Cisco Certified Technician)** = Introduction Certification highlighting support and maintenance of routers and switches. Persons with this certification can use the Cisco Internetwork Operating System and the Cisco Command Line Interface (CLI). Classification of IP Addressing, subnetting and security are also aspects of this certification.
- **CCENT (Cisco Certified Entry-Level Networking Technician)** = These professionals have the ability service and maintain small enterprise networks and have a familiarity with basic network security. Objectives for this certification include network technology fundamentals, security and wireless concepts, routing and switching. The exam for the CCENT is also 50% of the exams required for the CCNA certification.

- **CCNA (Cisco Certified Network Associate)** This certification is designed to assess the skills of Network Administrator and Engineers with 1-3 years of experience. The objectives of the exam(s) include the ability to configure, operate and troubleshoot various network technologies in a medium to large sized network environments. To gain this certification, it is possible to take either one exam or a two-part exam (Passing the first exam renders a person a CCENT, passing the 2nd exam will render a person also a CCNA.

- **MTA = (Microsoft Technology Associate also know as an "MCP" – Microsoft Certified Professional).** This certification is sponsored by Microsoft and based on networking software implementations. A person attempting an MTA would be well versed in "Operating Systems". Options for MTA at the time of writing this book included Windows 10, Server 2012, SQL Server, Exchange 2016, etc. Objectives for MTA-related examinations include assessing a person's understanding of network topologies, hardware, protocols, services and the OSI Model

- **MCSA or MCSE (Microsoft Certified Solutions Associate and Microsoft Certified Systems Engineer)** = These certifications are achieved when a person takes 4 or more certification examinations in a specific order. The collections of exams include higher-order functions of the Windows operating system including aspects such as: Active Directory, Domain Name System, Group Policy, Remote Access, VPN's and Data Security and many other network services.

How to earn a Network Technology Certification:

There are many certifications which indicate various levels of knowledge in Network Technology. This text seeks to offer the foundation knowledge which would supplement a program of study for those desiring to achieve some of those network technology certifications. At the time of the writing of this book, the following are some of the certifications available in the field of network technology:

- **Self-Study and Simulators:**
    - In order to get certified, there are no mandated courses, colleges or training programs. In fact, many certified people have never taken a computer class. Essentially, they were "Self-Taught" after locating resources which would allow them to accumulate

the knowledge to pass specific certification examinations. Suggested resources would be the following:

> **Simulators** = These are a practical tool which allow practicing many high-order tasks required in network technology. There is no "best" software for each has features which might be advantages for some certifications while not necessary for others. Some simulation software titles would include the following:

- Boson NetSim (Boson.com)
- Packet Tracer (Cisco.com)
- GNS3 (GNS3.com)
- CCIE Lab Builder (Cisco.com)
- Virtual Box (Oracle.com)

> **Certification Textbooks** = These are produced by many different publishers. The book you are presently reading is actually an example of the type used to earn certification. Due to the many authors in computer technology,..it would be difficult to say which book is the "best" but there are some methods you can use to select the books which are best for your certification endeavors. The following are a few ideas:

- Talk to technology professionals who have certifications. They can tell you which books and/or simulation software they used to pass the exams.
- Ask "technology training" programs which books they use. Often time you can purchase the books without taking the classes.
- Certification Organization Websites (i.e., "Comptia.com", "Microsoft.com" and "Cisco.com" often have links to books recommended for certifications. Be sure to check which numbers are associated with each exam prior to purchasing the books. Often books are sold which are associated with "old" and "Outdated" exams which are still using the same name.

- **Network Technology Training Schools:**

o Presently, there are many "For-Profit" institutions which have training programs and even degrees advertised as either "Network Technology Certificates" and even "Network Technology Degrees". Often times, these schools are called "Career Training Education (CTE)" institutions. These programs possess a broad variety of learning objectives and standards. When selecting a network technology program, do research on what standards they use to create the program. Questions such as the following would be beneficial when evaluating a potential program:

> What colleges or universities will accept the classes and credits from this program?
> What is the cost for this program compared to other schools both "For-Profit" and "Not-For-Profit"?
> What standards were used to establish the program?
> What organizations accredit the program?
> Please show me your job placement statistics?
> Am I allowed to re-take classes for free after completion of the program to keep skills up to date?

- **Two and Four-Year Colleges and Universities:**
  o Over the last 10 years, many colleges and universities have created "Network Technology" programs. The advantage to these colleges is that they also confer college degrees which would make a person more marketable in the technology field. In addition, having a degree allows a person to apply for other jobs outside of the field of network technology if they decided to change careers or needed employment until that perfect "Technology" job becomes available.

There are many institutions available which offer outstanding training experiences. Their costs range from free to extremely expensive, however. Do your research and balance out elements such as your available time and finances. Often times, certificate programs are a good place for basic understanding with the expectation that industry wide certification may follow in the future.

Recommendation on Correct Order to Take Certification Examinations:

Although it is not a requirement, having more than one certification is highly advantageous to a network professional. Multiple certifications will show perspective employers that a technician is an expert in many areas. If a technician had both a MCP and a CCENT, they know this person can both create a network and repair all the computers which are attached to the network. Many persons in the network technology field have a perspective on which examinations should be taken first and the particular order in which they should be attempted. There is no concrete document for most certifications attempts but there are some practical theories on the process. When planning on which certification(s) to take and their correct order,..give thought to the following:

- **What jobs do you have interest?** = If a person wants to work on networks and has no desire to repair computers,..there is no need to take the A+. Simply stick with examinations such as "Net+", "CCENT", etc.
- **Which certification will make later certifications easier to achieve?** = Many certifications have similar objectives. Examples of similar test objectives would be such as the following certifications which all have similar questions:
  - Net+
  - CCT
  - CCENT.

Taking examinations which have similar subject matter will make future examinations easier. It is like studying once to pass three different tests. There is no definite order of examinations at the lower levels of certification. Simply select the exams that will benefit you the greatest in the smallest amount of time.

Network Technology Groups and Organizations:

In addition to the specifics and details of connecting network devices, there are a number of "theories" and "Concepts" which are not "hands-on" elements. Prior to many of the technologies used in network design, there were many groups and organizations which discussed methods of communication, terms and standards. Many of these organizations are the primary contact point for network technologies and many of their discussions have become the standards used worldwide. The following terms reflect some of the groups and theories which are highly utilized and well known in the field of network technology:

- **RFC** = (Request for Comments) is the general name for a document which is disseminated and discussed by multiple groups and organizations. These organizations are normally international and reflect primary groups of representatives in various areas of technology. Examples would be the Institute of Electrical and Electronics Engineer (IEEE) and the International Organization for Standardization (ISO). Each organization modifies the document, adding and subtracting statements, descriptions and categories. After an agreed amount of time, the organizations vote on the RFC and it is adopted as a "Standard". A "Standard" is a recommendation on how a product, function or activity should occur. It is not a legal rule, simply a guideline implemented to increase clarity and to reduce the amount of documentation which would have to accompany a product. The guidelines are then published by groups such as the Internet Engineering Task Force (IETF) and the Internet Society (ISOC), two of the primary organizations which establish standards for internet and computer technology communications. Some examples of RFC's include the following:

Request for Comment Examples	
RFC 20	ASCII format for network interchange
RFC 1518	Address allocation with CIDR
RFC 1542	DHCP/BOOTP complient routers
RFC 792	Internet control message protocol
RFC 1034	Domain names - concepts and facilities
RFC 1058	Routing information protocol
RFC 1459	Internet relay chat protocol

- **ISO** = (International Organization for Standardization) is an independent, non-governmental international organization based in Geneva, Switzerland. The participants of the ISO are considered to be experts who share knowledge and develop voluntary international standards to support innovation, consistency and global solutions to various worldwide situations. The members include over 161 national groups who all discuss, devise and develop standards for products, services and systems concerning quality and safety. There are over 21,000 International Standards and related ISO documents ranging from technology, food, energy, waste and many other areas. There are two primary models of communications in networking which are advocated by the ISO:

- o **OSI Model (Open Source Interconnect)** = A conceptual description listing the elements of network devices and how they communicate. This model separates network communication, software and devices into 7 distinct layers. Each layer supports specific functions which in turn allow transition into layers either above or below it. Without going into detail, the following are the seven layers of the OSI model and some of the related features within the layer:

OPEN SOURCE INTERCONNECT (OSI-MODEL)				
LAYER#	NAME	FUNCTION	ASSOCIATION	PDU TYPE
7	APPLICATION	File transfer, e-mail	Browsers ms-outlook	DATA
6	PRESENTATION	Formats data for transfer	Ansi, oem, etc.	DATA
5	SESSION	Creates and coordinates connections between applications		DATA
4	TRANSPORT	Data flow and error correction	Tcp, udp	SEGMENT
3	NETWORK	Establishes communication path between nodes	Routers	PACKET
2	DATA	Conversion to bits	Switches	FRAME
1	PHYSICAL	Carries the bits	Hubs, nic's, cables	BIT
WAYS TO REMEMBER LAYERS ORDER (First letter of each word represents layer:				
ALL PIMPS SELECT THE NICE DIAMOND PIECES				
ALL PEOPLE SEEM TO NEED DATA PROCESSING				
PLEASE DO NOT THROW SAUSAGE PIZZA AWAY				

- o **TCP/IP Model (Originally called the DOD model)** = This communication model separates network communications into 4 layers. Essentially, this model predates the OSI model and did not originally include much "software" related specifications (In the 60's, there were no applications such as "Firefox" and "Microsoft Word" so most communication technology was related to hardware). As time progressed, layers representing software were encompassed in the higher levels of the TCP/IP model. Below is a representation of the TCP/IP model as related to the OSI model:

TCP/IP MODEL		
LAYER#	NAME	FUNCTION
4	APPLICATION	FTP, Telnet, e-mail, DNS
3	TRANSPORT (HOST-TO-HOST)	Formats data for transfer
2	INTERNET	Creates and coordinates connections between applications
1	NETWORK	Data flow and error correction

- **IEEE (Institute of Electrical and Electronics Engineer)** = Members include thousands of professionals working in the field of electronics, networking, computers and overall science technology. With its beginning in about 1844, IEEE is often considered to be the world's largest technical "Think Tank". Some of the standards implemented by IEEE include the following:

IEEE Standards	
Section Name	**Brief Reference Description**
IEEE 802.1	Higher Layer LAN Protocols
IEEE 802.2	LLC

IEEE 802.3	Ethernet
IEEE 802.4	Token bus
IEEE 802.5	Token ring MAC layer
IEEE 802.6	MAN's
IEEE 802.7	Broadband LAN using Coaxial Cable
IEEE 802.8	Fiber Optic TAG
IEEE 802.9	Integrated Services LAN
IEEE 802.10	Interoperable LAN Security
IEEE 802.11	Wireless LAN (WLAN) & Mesh (Wi-Fi certification)
IEEE 802.12	100BaseVG
IEEE 802.13	None according to records
IEEE 802.14	Cable modems
IEEE 802.15	Wireless PAN
IEEE 802.15.1	Bluetooth certification

Chapter 2
Network Topologies

Network Topologies:

This term identifies the anticipated design or the existing arrangement of devices on a network. Servers, cables, rooms, routers, switches and many other devices can be included in the layout of the network topology. Often times, different parts of the network may be evaluated in a manner which requires only specific elements of the network to be displayed. When this occurs, a subset of a topology is created called a "Network Decomposition" which filters out anything extraneous to the aspects of the network elements under evaluation. At the root levels, there are two essential levels of a network topology. Those would be the "Logical" topology and the "Physical" topology.

- **Logical** = This network decomposition lists the identities of network devices in groups. Presently, an accepted standard is to utilize the IP addresses of nodes and hosts in reference to their associations and establishing which part of the network in which the device resides. Additional descriptions and symbols identifying items such as firewalls, e-mail servers and domain controllers often accompany many of the characteristics of a Logical Topology. Below are some examples:

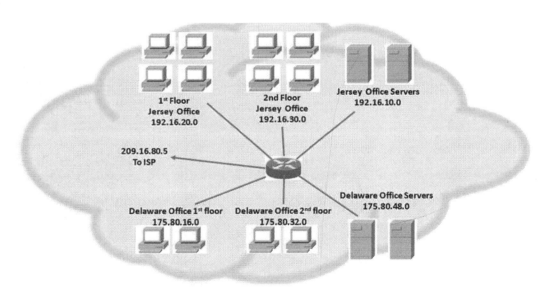

Company WAN example

- **Physical** = This network composition identities how devices are physically connected to one another based on cables, wireless and other connection media. There are characteristics of actual distance and proximity of devices. In addition, the arrangement of media connections are also highlighted on physical topologies which results in various names for specific designs. Below are some examples of Physical Topologies:

> **LAN (Local Area Network)** = Network which includes communication connected computers within close proximity of one another such as a room or building.

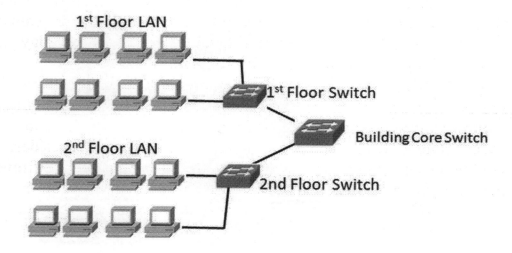

> **MAN (Metropolitan (or "Medium") Area Network))** = Collection of connected LANS spanning the territory of a complex, campus or city.
> **WAN (Wide Area Network)** = This network is a collection of connected MANS which are separated by large geographic distances such as in state to state or country to country. One of the best examples of a WAN is the internet.
> **BUS** = Network setup in which each computer and network device are connected to a single cable or backbone. This topology was the standard during the beginning of most company and building networks. The primary disadvantage to a bus network was in the fact that if a single break was on the line, all network communication would cease.

> **RING** = A circular design for a network in which a PDU travels from one node to the next in a specific sequence. In the early implementations of this topology, the PDU only traveled in a single direction. If there was a single break in the line,..all communications would stop.

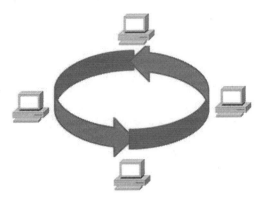

> **STAR** = Using a "Central Point" for communications, all nodes are connected via the central point which is often a hub or a switch. The PDU travels independently of the number of nodes and the failure of any node will not disrupt the others. The single disadvantage in this typology is that the central point is very critical if it fails, the entire network will not operate.

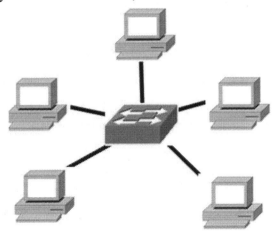

> **MESH** = This topology is the most stable. Essentially, every node has more than one connection to all the other nodes. Using this connection style,.the network can continue operating with multiple failures in connection lines or nodes. The primary disadvantage to this topology is the redundancy increases the cost of the network due to the duplicated lines and devices.

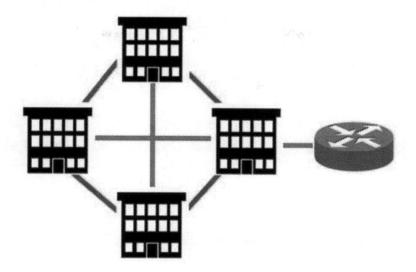

Setup and Configuration of Network Devices

The bases for most network communications are established around interfaces, addressing and protocols. Prior to any of the aforementioned elements communicating, network devices must be manually configured. While minor network devices (i.e., hubs and small home network technology) requires no interaction from a user other than turning it on, corporate-level network technology requires a skilled technician to initiate sessions, test bandwidth and troubleshoot data disconnects on a daily basis. The following paragraphs give an overview regarding the processes involved with configuring and connecting network devices.

- **Connection methods** = There many methods of connecting Switches and Routers. Which method is chosen totally depends on the network technology involved and the background of the network technician. Below are some of the tools and software used by persons in the network technology field:
  - **Console Cable (Rolled)** = A cable which often looks "Flat" is connected to a computers serial port (Often called a "Com" port) while the other end is inserted into a router or a switch. Because of network standards,..the color of this type of cable is often "light blue" or "black" (Black cables attempt to identify the fact that these cables can also fit and be used in the "Auxiliary" port on a router or switch.

o **USB Console Cable** = This cable is similar to the rolled console cable in color and flatness but the ends (Terminators) on the cable have USB interfaces on one or both ends.

o **IP-Based network** = When corporate-level (Not "Small Office Home Office (SOHO)") routers and switches are first taken out of their boxes as "new" they have no settings which would allow them to communicate on a network. After a console cable has been used to configure options like passwords and IP address, a network device can be configured without being in physical proximity of the device. Essentially, if the device is connected to your cooperate network (i.e., LAN, MAN or WAN) or anywhere on the internet, a tech would be able to connect to the device using it's IP address combined with one of the management software listed below.

- **Network Management Software** = In order to configure and monitor the functions on network devices there is required a software interface. The software selected can provide access to multiple capabilities of a network device. Which management software selected can be either proprietary or the preference of a network technician. Below are some of the options available concerning management software:

o **Web Browser** = There are many varieties of web browsers such as "Chrome", Firefox", "Internet Explorer", "Safari", etc. Many manufacturers install "Web Server" control features into their network devices which allow access to the device simply by typing the device's IP address into the browser. Oftentimes, when using a browser, the browser interface is called a "WebUI" (Web User Interface). Various "Buttons" and "Icons" are used to activate or engage device services and functions. The advantage to using a browser is that no additional software is required to access a network device. In addition, as long as the device is on a network and has electricity, a connection can be initiated from any device which has a browser (i.e., laptop, cellphone, IP-based television, etc.). Unfortunately, utilizing a browser requires that a device has been configured with basic configurations (i.e., IP address, passwords, etc.). In addition, depending on the manufacture, all of the devices features might not be available.

o **HyperTerminal** = This is one of the oldest software's used for configuring network devices. It was based upon using telephone modems. Using HyperTerminal, a laptop or desktop and a console cable, a technician is able to turn on a "Command Line Interface" (Also called "CLI" and looks like what is classically called "DOS") = Access to HyperTerminal between 1995 and 2006 was extremely easy. The software is a free download and came included with many operating systems. The software required no installation so it could be run off of any device from a folder. prompt). Using the CLI it is possible to configure all features because the majority of network technology devices are customized for CLI commands. In the later years,..other updated configuration software was released to compensate for the lack of security features in HyperTerminal.

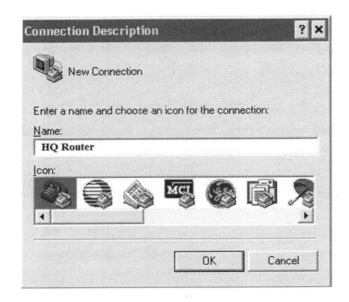

o **Teraterm** = This package has all the functions of HyperTerminal but many other enhancements. The user interface offers options concerning size of font, colors, tabbed views and many other superficial elements. In addition, there are many features critical in network device management such as Secure Shell (Called "SSH") which creates levels of encryption and security and Trivial File Transfer Protocol options (Called "TFTP") which allows the backup of configurations or the easy upload of the device operating systems. This allows use of configuration thru telnet, hypertext Transmission Protocol and the Console connection.

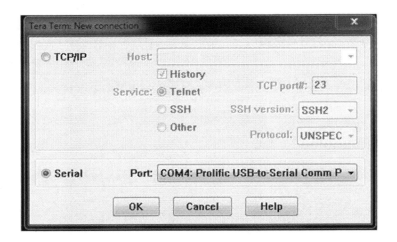

o **Telnet** – Very popular during the initial growth and installation of network technology. This allows configuration of a network device using a command line interface embedded in many computer operating systems. Using unique commands, as long as the device could be "pinged" (Contacted) on a network via its IP address, using a CLI, a technician could perform almost all functions on network devices. A disadvantage to telnet is that it requires a "Server" and "Client" component to be installed and activated on both the access computer and the network device. In addition, the device would have to have already been configured with and IP address, passwords and other login information. In addition, telnet transmits information in what is termed as "Cleartext" which means that all typed commands sent between the computer and network device can be easily captured and "literally" read to discover passwords and other important data.

- o **Putty** = A free, open-source software used to configure varies network devices. In addition to provide multiple configuration, file transfer and encryption abilities. It provides other functions concerning encryption, compression and remote desktop.

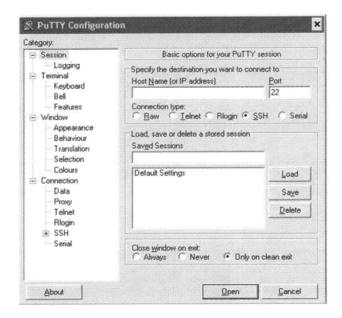

What is a Client Computer?

A "Client" performs all of the functions of a "Workstation" with a few special modifications. A "Client" requests services, access, or permissions from another network device called a "Server". Essentially, a client computer must ask a "Server" for approval for many of the functions a user might attempt on that client. For example,..many clients require a user to input a "username" and "Password" prior to using the client. When the username and password are typed by the user and the "enter" key is pressed,..that information is sent to a "Server" for approval. If the Server has knowledge of the username and password combination, a message is sent to the "client" approving the user and then the user's computer will activate. If the user does not exist, or if the user's account is turned off,..a "deny" message is sent to the client which prohibits the user's access to the computer. The following are other services a client must request:

- Connection settings for a business network.
- Access to the internet.
- Permission to access printers.
- Permission to access files on network devices.
- Access to secured databases.

What is a Server?

In network technology, a "Server" is a system that "Gives out Stuff" or "Approvals". There are many type of servers in operation such as the following:

- DHCP Servers giving network configurations for workstations, phones and laptops.
- Web servers which hold and display websites.
- Video Services which allow access to movies online.
- Email servers for transmitting and receiving texts and documents.
- Security Servers which allow user access via usernames and passwords.
- Domain Name Servers which allow users to find internet websites using a friendly name.

Selected Concepts, Devices and Signals in Network Technology:

In the field of network technology, there are a number of terms utilized for descriptions, settings and configuration. Prior to the exploration of the different technologies, it will be helpful to give a brief overview of a few of the concepts a person will encounter and have to manipulate. The following are a few of the terms and explanations which will be discussed in this text:

- **Bandwidth** = This term describes the maximum amount of data which can exist on a connection at the same time. Contemporary network devices operate at one of four speeds: 10, 100, 1000 or 10,000 Mbps. If devices of different speeds are directly connected the "faster" port will reduce its speed to match the speed of the "slower" port. Please note,..although the speeds are very distinct,..an active connection only uses a portion of the available port speed. Think of it as a garden hose which has a "trickle" of water passing thru it at one time while other times the faucet is fully turned on and the entire inside of the hose is filled with water traveling towards the spout.
- **Protocol Data Units** = Depending on the type of network and software in use,..technicians will describe the "message pieces" differently. Networks have equipment which requires the messages to be formatted in many different ways to be compatible with other network devices. Below are some of the more widely used terms to describing network technology messages along with generic descriptions to be expanded upon later:
  - ➤ **Packets** = Small information units. Very fast and compatible with multiple types of networks.

- ➢ **Frames** = Think of a frame as a collection of "packets" in a container. The container allows groups of packets to have rules of travel and elements of security to protect the data.
- ➢ **Cells** = Imagine this as a bubble or circle which carries large amounts of data. Cells were used on older networks and recent Video-Related networks because the data was more reliable concerning arriving at destinations.
- ➢ **Tokens** = This would be regarded as a "Cell" with rules. A Token is configured to travel in a specific direction between intermediate destinations arranged on a network. The token always uses the same path and often has path-redundancy in case the primary route is cut or damaged.

- **"Amount" units and "Speeds" in networks** = There are many descriptions which attempts to define maximum amount of data with the longest time it takes for a message unit to travel from a source to a destination. This is specified by the type of technology the message is using to travel. There are various types of networks technology, each with specific distance advantages and limitations. In this book, we include discussions which reflect the following speed format:
  - ➢ bps = Bits per second.
  - ➢ Kbps = Kilobits per second (Equal to 1000bps).
  - ➢ Mbps = Megabits per second (Equal to 1000kbps).
  - ➢ Gbps = Gigabits per second (Equal to 1000Mbps).
- **Transmission Types** = Essentially, there are two general signal forms which are illustrated and measured differently:
  - ➢ **Broad Band** = The measure of this form normally is illustrated with a smooth curving line which rises and falls like a "camel's back". This is measured using a concept called "Frequency". Frequency is the time that passes before an event occurs as well as the position of the line between the occurrences. The carrier for broadband is normally light waves or sound waves.
  - ➢ **Base Band** = The measure of this form is illustrated by using sharp, straight lines which travel up or down with pauses traveling from left to right. Think of this as something which looks like a "Picket Fence" or the top of the chess game piece called a "Rook". The carrier for this type of signal is often electrical "pops" that register as either "on" or "off".
- **VoIP Phones** = Instead of using a system called "POTS (Plain old Telephone System)" which requires the installation of telephone lines,

there are technologies which allow telephones to be connected to traditional computer networks. These phones use the same software which allows computers to interact with networks. The networks which accept these type of phones are often referred to as "Voice over Internet Protocol" networks. Many telecommunication companies include VoIP as services they offer such as Vonage, Comcast, Cisco and others.

- **Network-based computers** = In order to store and retrieve data on the internet requires the use of computers called "Servers". These computers hold and display movies, text, photos and many other products and services used in the world. We also discuss a type of computer called a "client" or "workstation". Clients are simply computer-related devices which primarily access the data on servers. Examples of clients would be your home computer or a Smartphone.

- **Hubs** = This device is one of the oldest used in networks. This device essentially multiplies physical connections to a network. For example, if there is normally a single connection which leads to the internet in a building. The hub would allow multiple devices access to this single connection. The devices could be computers, printers, or even video cameras. We normally classify hubs as "legacy devices". A legacy device is something that is based upon older technology but is still often used today. When selecting to use a Hub on a network, there are a few "Pros" and "Cons" which should be considered:

  - ➤ **Pros:**
    1. **Inexpensive** = Hubs are often sold for under $60 dollars for small home offices.
    2. **Easy to use** = No configuration required. Simply plug in the ports and electricity and they operate.
    3. **Widely available** = Due to the number of years they have been around, they can be found thru any network technology supplier.
  - ➤ **Cons:**
    1. **Divides bandwidth** = Each device you plug in will reduce the bandwidth the hub is rated to support. Take the following example:
       a. A hub which operates at 10Mbps has 10 available ports.
          i. If two devices are connected,...the hub now runs at 5Mbps.

ii. If ten devices are connected,..the hub now runs at 1Mbps.

2. **Requires close physical proximity for repair** = Traditionally, there is no way to access, maintain or repair a standard, base-model hub unless you can touch it. If a person's office is on the 4th floor of a building but the connection leads to the hub in the basement,..someone will have to walk to the basement to address the hubs fault.

3. **Single-port signal** = Essentially one unit of data can pass thru the hub at a given time (Please note that this is in "milliseconds"). While that single data unit passes thru a single port in the hub, no other transmissions can occur on the other ports.

- **Switches** = This device operates much like a hub except it compensates for some of the disadvantages associated with hubs. The prices for switches range from moderate to extremely expensive (Some models cost $8,000.00 or more). The following are some aspects concerning switches:

  ➢ **Multiplies network connections** = One port is normally connected to the network while dozens of others are connected to other network devices (Hubs, Switches, etc.) or computer systems (Servers, clients, printers, phones, etc.).

  ➢ **Dedicated bandwidth** = No bandwidth is divided due to connected devices. Regardless the number of physical connections, switches will maintain the bandwidth for which they are rated.

  ➢ **Multiple lines of simultaneous communications** = Switches allow multiple signals or communications to travel thru the devices at essentially the same time.

  ➢ **Remote access** = A switch can be configured to allow connections from anywhere in the world as long as it has an ip address and electricity being supplied. There are multiple methods of "remote access" utilized on switches and other network devices.

  ➢ **Network Segmentation** = Mid-range and higher switches have the ability to separate and segregate section of a network. This process is called "VLANs (Virtual Local Area Networks)". Some VLAN implementations are for the following:

1. **Security** = Assuring specific groups of computers cannot interact with other computers (i.e., student computers versus teacher computers).
2. **Bandwidth conservation** = A single computer uploading or downloading large files can hamper a network. If you segment the network with VLANs, only computers on that particular VLAN would be hampered. Operations on the other computers would occur because they do not know the other VLANs exist.

- **Routers** = These network devices are the primary connection points of the internet. Essentially, each building which has an internet connection normally has all of the switches connected in series terminating into a Router. The router provides the connection to an Internet Service Provider (ISP) which is connected to the internet backbone (Really the Department of Defense for which every country you presently reside). In addition to the primary internet connection, Routers also provide the following functions:
  - ➤ **Remote access** = A Router can be configured to allow connections from anywhere in the world as long as it has an ip address and electricity being supplied. There are multiple methods of "remote access" utilized on routers and other network devices.
  - ➤ **Filtering** = Signals on the internet constantly travel and will attempt to flow into networks for which they are not destined. Routers will block any communications which attempt to access a network in which the desired target does not exist.
  - ➤ **Traffic Flow** = The internet is a large, complicated set of interconnected pathways. Routers can learn the fastest routes between sending and receiving devices. In addition, when a pathway fails, routers have the ability to negotiate with other routing devices to find other ways to destinations. Routers are often regarded as the "Traffic Cops" of the internet.

Chapter 3
Signals, Cables and Connections

Signals, Cables and Connections:

All network devices are connected in some format. The actual connections are all over the world. Sometimes deep underground, some undersea and others going well above the earth to return to a remote destination. The various network connections use metal wires, "glass-like" fibers while others can communicate through the air without being physically connected. In conversations concerning network technology another way of saying "connection type" is "media" or "medium". Various media has different connectors, lengths, advantages and disadvantages. The following are some of the media used in various types of networks.

- **Network Interface Card (NIC)** = This term often describes the internal portion on a computer which controls connections to a network through the use of some type of connection media which could be metal, fiber or wireless.
- **Port** = This term describes the connection point into a NIC or interface on switch or router.
- **Coax** = (Short for "Coaxial Cable") is one of the oldest network technology media. This cable has been used since the late 60's. More recently Coax is used primarily in visual implementations such as CCTV (Closed Circuit Television). A version of it is also used by some cable television carriers to connect a home modem or "Home Router" to the demarc in the house (The hole in the wall which connects to your ISP (Internet Service Provider). Coax comes in the two following versions:
  - ➢ **ThickNet** = Cabling of this type is older and not used frequently. It can be found connecting older buildings within corporate complexes, libraries or universities. Thicknet is about 1/2 inch in diameter and one of its major disadvantages was that it was not very flexible. The primary transmission speed most Thicknet networks achieved was up to 10 Mbps with a maximum single length of no more than 500 meters (Approximately 1,640 feet). Thicknet is often referred to as 10Base5 (The maximum distance of a segment equals 500 meters so it was agreed upon to drop the last two zeros).
  - ➢ **ThinNet** = ThinNet resembles the type of wire which is often used to connect home subscriber's television to cable boxes TV. ThinNet coax is about 1/4 inch in diameter and is more flexible then ThickNet. The longest span of a ThinNet cable is 185 meters (607 ft.). When describing this cable, it is often

referred to as 10Base2 (Persons in the field desired to "abbreviate" the name for the technology. Since the maximum distance is 185 meters, it was agreed upon to "round the 185 up" to "200" and then drop the two zeros). This type of network media uses a connector called a "BNC (British Navel Connector).

- **Category Cable (Also called Twisted Pair or "Cat")** = Cable of this type is what we often see connected to telephones or basic network devices. The normal distance limitation of category cable is about 100 meters (Approximately 328 feet). The other name. "twisted-pair" originates from the construction of the cable. Within the cable, there are multiple-pairs of wires which are twisted in parallel (Side-by-side). There are many definitions concerning twisted pair cabling. One definition is based on the material used in the cable creation. Below appear the three primary material types:
  - ➢ **Shielded Twisted Pair (STP)** = Metallic foil surrounds the twisted wire pairs within the cable. The foil increases protection against electromagnetic interference which allows for faster data transmissions. STP is sometimes more expensive due to its composition and devices which might be required to provide better protection against EMI such as termination and grounding.
  - ➢ **Unshielded Twisted (UTP)** = Cable of this type has layer of material specifically provided for protection. It is often the type of cable viewed directly connected to computers from a hub or a switch.
  - ➢ **Plenum-Rated** = This type of cable incorporates special materials in the cable covering. The makeup of the cable includes flame-retardant synthetics and low smoke materials to provide increased resistance against fire or the emission of toxic gasses.
- **Different versions of category cable have numbers which indicate their use. Below are some of the category types:**
  - ➢ **Cat-1 thru 3** = Primarily telephones and older basic technology.
  - ➢ **Cat-4** = Supported speeds of 16 Mbps
  - ➢ **Cat-5** = Supports speeds of between 10/100 Mbps (Called "FastEthernet).
  - ➢ **Cat-5e** = Supports speeds of 1000 Mbps speeds (Called Gigabit Ethernet)

- ➢ **Cat-6** = It's suitable for up to 10 gigabit Ethernet (Called "10GigE) and has an internal separator between pairs of wires to protect from signal crosstalk (Signals from one set of wires interfering with signals on other wires).
- **Category cable in network technology have two primary terminators or connectors with the following names:**
  - ➢ **RJ-45 (Registered Jack #45)** = Network device connector.
  - ➢ **RJ-11 (Registered Jack #11)** = Primary connector with telephones.
- **Fiber-Optic Cable** = This media is comprised of an almost hair thin material referred to as "Glass" which is encased in mirrored cladding and a protective outer sleeve. Essentially, signals of light travel thru fiber allowing incredibly fast speeds (Upwards of 10,000 Mbps). It also allows communications over long distances (2 kilometers and greater). Due to its construction fiber-optic cable is very expensive. Although there are many type of fiber-optic cable, two will receive attention in this text:
  - ➢ **Multi-mode** = 550 meters
  - ➢ **Single-Mode** = support runs between 2 meters and 10,000 meters
- **Connector types for fiber cable vary in construction** = Some types which might be found on a fiber-based network include the following:

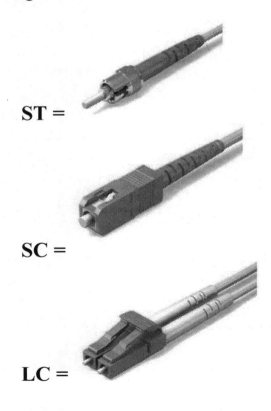

ST =

SC =

LC =

- **Wireless** = Wireless networks exist between nodes which use the "air" as a medium. Clients transmit and receive either "light/sound/or radio" waives for communication. Some popular wireless technologies are the following:
  - ➤ **Bluetooth** = Very popular connection technologies used in cars, cell phones, entertainment systems, etc. Bluetooth requires very little equipment and operates on very low power. The range for Bluetooth networks vary from 33 feet to 10 meters depending on the class device in use.
  - ➤ **NFC (Near Field Communication)** = NFC allows devices such as a smartphones, printers and computers to communicate. The primary limitation of NFC is the range. Basic NFC requires the devices to be within about 2 inches of each other for communication. This type of technology is often used to allow two cell phones to transmit data between them if they are held close together.
  - ➤ **802.11 Standards** = These are documents which discuss and illustrate recommended methods of wireless communications which were created by the Institute of Electrical and Electronics Engineers (IEEE) LAN/MAN Standards Committee (Also called "IEEE 802"). There are a number of versions of the "802.11" many of which began in the mid-1990's. Some of the more better-known standards include the following:

Standard	Frequency	Maximum Throughput	Distance (Radius)
802.11a	5 GHz	54 Mbit/s	115 feet (Obstruction limited)
802.11b	2.4 GHz	11 Mbit/s	115 feet
802.11g	2.4 GHz	54 Mbit/s	125 feet
802.11n	5GHz and/or 2.4GHz	300 Mbit/s	230 feet (Obstruction limited)

Combining Cable & Speed Technologies and their Descriptions:

Multiple types of technologies are combined for the functioning of most networks. Although people often use the term "Ethernet" cable,..understand that this is a technology "norm" and not a thoroughly complete descriptor. There are however, other terms used in technology which combines many aspects of how a network functions. These terms are actually technology field standards. The following is a brief description of some technologies prevalent in network technology:

- **10Base5** = Network which used RG-8 cable media about .50 inches in diameter with baseband transmissions of up to 10 megabits per second (Mbps). The primary connectors were called "AUI (Attachment User Interface)". The maximum distance between nodes is 500 meters (About 1,640 feet). Another name which was used for this type of network was "ThickNet". This is an older technology which is not used very often due to the materials being very expensive but can still be found as the "Backbone" cable on networks due to its durability and distance capacity.
- **10Base2** = Networks of this type use .25 thick RG-58A/U coaxial cable terminated with BNC connectors. The maximum speed is up to 10Mbps using baseband transmissions for a range of 185 meters (About 607 feet) per segment. A name used for this type of network was also "ThinNet". The "2" is intended to reflect the number "185" rounded up to "200" and dropping the last two zeros in order to make the description easier to pronounce.
- **10BaseT** = Using "Category" cable, these networks support 10 Mbps over two pairs of copper wires within a cable which can house multiple pairs of wires. The maximum segment is 100 meters (About 328 feet). This network type utilizes RJ-45 connectors. In this description the letter "T" represents that idea that the cable type uses very small wires "twisted" in pairs.
- **1000Base-T** = Using "Category" cable, these networks support either 10, 100, or 1000 Mbps over four pairs of highly twisted cable utilizing better copper and often times transistors in NIC's. The maximum segment is 100 meters (About 328 feet). This network type utilizes RJ-45 connectors. In this description the letter "T" represents that idea that the cable type uses very small wires "twisted" in pairs.
- **Hop (Or "Hop Count")** = Network term which describes the number of devices a PDU must travel through in order to arrive at its destination. Any device which makes a decision about which path messages take is included in a "hop count". Devices which have no routing abilities (i.e., hub, server, etc.) are not included in a hop count.

Protocols (Network Language for Communications):

Regardless of what type of device is on a network, there must be software to allow it to be managed and to allow it to communicate. The names of some of these software's are often used to describe what makes up the primary communication standard of a network. The following protocol types below are some highlights of the software which allows networks to communicate:

- **NetBIOS (Network Basic Input/Output System)** = This protocol which allows software on computers to exchange information a local area network (LAN). Client identities are identified using alpha-numeric identities (0-9 and A-Z). Often identities were limited to 8 characters or less.
- **NetBeui (NetBIOS Extended User Interface)** = This is an older protocol used for DOS and original Window networks (Primarily Windows 3.10 and Windows 95) designed for a single LAN segment. The protocol will not allow communications between discontinuous networks.
- **WINS (Windows Internet Name Service)** = This associates NetBIOS names to IP addresses on a LAN. This software was run as a service on a server to allow clients to locate other clients which might be on other LAN segments. WINS alone is non-routable but the software can be "carried" within another protocol such as networks that use NetBIOS over TCP/IP (NetBT).
- **IPX/SPX (Internet Packet Exchange/Sequential Packet Exchange)** = This is a LAN communication protocol developed by one of the original companies for network communications known as Novell networks. This protocol uses hexadecimal identities (0-9 and A-F) for devices and cannot be routed on the internet.
- **TCP/IP (Transmission Control Protocol/Internet Protocol)** = Method for communications between computers on small and large networks. The protocol is actually a combination TCP/IP is a combination of two protocols suites verbally separated for easier explanation. Each suite is a combination of protocols but they have the same purposes as in the following:
  - o **Transmission Control Protocol (TCP)** = Attempts to assure the dependable transmission of data between networks and devices. Within this capacity, the protocol will attempt to correct for data errors and requests re-transmissions of lost data.
  - o **Internet Protocol (IP)** = Attempts to define the path that data, signals, packets, pdu's, etc., will take to travel between a sending device and destination.
- **IPv4 (Internet Protocol Version 4)** = The primary protocol in data communication over different kinds of networks. This protocol identifies network devices by a 12-character decimal identity separated into 4

sections (192.168.1.1). Using this system allowed a worldwide network with over four billion IP addresses. With the increase of internet-connected devices (i.e., cell phones, car and home security, etc.) however, there is the potential of running out of IP's which can be accessed over the internet. Due to the address limitation, networks presently use other identity methods including IPv6, CIDR and VLSM (Terms will be explained and described later in this text).

- **IPv5 (Known as "Internet Streaming Protocol")** = This was primarily used for transmitting video and direct communication between routing devices for services for routing. Extremely fast and robust with multiple applications but requires high-end network devices for implementation.

- **IPv6 (Internet Protocol v6)** = This utilizes a combination of 32 hexadecimal characters for the identity of network devices. An example of an IPv6 identity would be "fe80::75ea:6ec0:e6f8:f037". This method allows close to 340 undecillion available IP addresses. IPv6 also understands communications from IPv4 devices. Unfortunately, IPv4 devices cannot understand communications directly from IPv6 networks unless there is a software or device between the different networks to provide data conversion.

- **DHCP (Dynamic Host Configuration Protocol)** = This protocol gives identities to network devices in the form of an IPv4 address. The protocol will also provide network settings so network devices can find networks outside of the specific LAN. DHCP also attempts to assure that duplicated IP addresses are not given out to multiple network devices which could cause an entire network to stop functioning.

- **DNS (Domain Name System (or Service or Server))** = This associates domain names into IP addresses. Whenever someone wants to go to "Disney.com" the request goes to DNS servers around the world. Those servers have a "Shared list" which includes all known domains linked to IP addresses. Once the domain is found in the DNS server, the IP address is sent to the computer which requested the domain. The computer then uses that address to get to the desired domain.

- **Telnet** = This is a protocol which uses a "Command Line Interface" which allows connection to network devices (Routers, Switches, Computers, etc.) over vast TCP/IP distances. Options for use include browsing directors and limited "Text-based" control over devices. Although very effective, telnet is highly unsecure for PDU's are easily read with widely available software.

- **SSH (Secure Shell)** = This protocol allows authentication and hides (Also called "Encrypts") communications between two or more devices when connected over some public or less-secure environments like the Internet. Many network administrators use this for remotely accessing network systems and computers in order to perform commands or transmit and receive files.
- **SMTP (Simple Mail Transfer Protocol)** = This is used to transfer e-mail messages between e-mail servers. On some networks, it is also used to send mail from an e-mail client (i.e., Microsoft Outlook) to an e-mail server.
- **POP (Post Office Protocol)** = This is used to retrieve e-mail from a mail server. Many e-mail applications on computers and smart phones use POP. The primary versions of POP require that the original version of the e-mail is moved between the server and the client which might result in a loss of stored e-mail if the server or client were to stop working.
- **IMAP (Internet Message Access Protocol)** = This allows users email to be stored on the actual e-mail server while allowing the user to create folders and organize the items as if they existed on the user's computer. E-mail is protected against a client failure because the data actually resides on the e-mail server.
- **FTP (File Transfer Protocol)** = This is used to move files between computers. This is what occurs in the background when photos or other files are posted to online services such as "Facebook" or "ITunes". This is a robust protocol which checks each "part" of a file to make sure the total file has no errors in transmission.
- **HTTP (Hypertext Transfer Protocol)** = This allows network devices to display text, graphic images, sound, video, and other multimedia files on applications known as "Browsers" (i.e., Internet Explorer, Chrome, Safari, etc.).
- **HTTPS (Hypertext Transfer Protocol Secure also called "Secure Sockets")** = This is used for sensitive data and transactions such as billing, credit cards transactions, user login and many other processes where security of data is required. The protocol "scrambles" the data being transmitted so it is difficult to read if captured by some other device or person. In addition, it attempts to create a more dedicated private connection between a user's web browser and the web server. Often times, HTTPS can be combined with many other security options such as web or e-mail certifications.

- **TFTP (Trivial File Transfer Protocol)** = This is a protocol and software suite used for moving small files between devices which do not have overhead or the need for security or authentication.
- **RDP (Remote Desktop Protocol)** = This allows a user to access a system without the need for being physically in the same location as the device. It is often used by various tech support services. Essentially, a person can sit anywhere in the world and interact with a computer as if they were setting directly in front of the computer. This protocol also enables a number of features of assistance to most computer or network devices interaction such as the following:
  - ➢ Mouse and keyboard
  - ➢ Data encryption
  - ➢ Audio, printer and file redirection
  - ➢ Clipboard sharing between a remote server and a local client

Chapter 4
Internet and other Network Interoperability Terms and Methods

Internet and other Network Interoperability Terms and Methods:

WWW (World Wide Web) = The term "Internet" is now used synonymously with WWW but there is an essential difference. Think of the "Internet" as a "large book" with many pages and chapters. World Wide Web (or "WWW") is the "Table of Contents" used to locate the specific item in the book in which a person has interest in researching. This term describes a searchable information storage system which includes entries from all over the earth. The items in the information system could be as small as two or three sentences on a document to as large as books with thousands of pages. In addition to text-based information this global information resource includes videos, music, graphics and interactive systems used for both knowledge, education and entertainment. Some of the earliest implementations of the World Wide Web are attributed to the work of Tim Berners-Lee as recently as 1989. He compiled code which allowed access to the global bank of knowledge known as WWW via using code such as HTML (Hypertext Markup Language), URLs (Uniform Resource Locators) communication protocols such as HTTP (Hypertext Transfer Protocol) and internet browsers (Netscape Navigator, Internet Explorer, Mozilla Firefox and Google Chrome).

URL (Also called a "Uniform Resource Locator") = This item is best referenced as "Whatever a person types in a browser to get to a website". Take "Facebook.com" for example. When a person desires to go to Facebook, those are the words they place in the top of most browsers (That area is called an "Address Bar".). The address "Facebook" is not a single server on the internet. It reflects dozens of servers owned by Facebook to provide their services. A "URL (Uniform Resource Locator)" has the same purpose as a UNC (Universal Naming Convention) in that it is used to locate a file or program stored on a network device. The primary difference is in that a URL normally references a resource on a network other than the network the user is located within. Traditionally, this "other network" is a different company or an item on a server located somewhere on the internet. Although the purpose of both UNC's and URL's are identical, the elements and characters in a URL are different. URL (Uniform Resource Locator) commands have what is often called a "Protocol Identifier" followed by a "Colon (:)." In addition, the "sections" in a URL are separated by the character often referred to as a "Forward slash (/)". Examples of Protocol Identifiers would be as follows:

- **HTTP** = Hypertext Protocol (Website display and viewing).
- **HTTPS** = Secure Hypertext Protocol (Protected internet transactions).
- **FTP** = File Transfer Protocol (For upload and download of files).

Another distinction for a URL is that the device identity is normally a "Fully Qualified Domain Name (FQDN)". This is the name of the server or group of servers which are registered with the internet. Each server or group of servers use a name followed by what is referred to as a "Top Level Domain (i.e., ".com", ".org", ".net", etc.)." Each server directly connected to the internet must be registered with a number of different organizations (i.e., Arpanet, Department of Defense, etc.). These organizations own DNS servers (Domain Name Servers) which are the "Table of Contents" or the "Phone Book" for the internet. Essentially, when anyone attempts to access a website, the request is first sent to a DNS server which looks for the name which had been typed in an address bar (i.e., "Google.com", "Facebook.com", etc.). The DNS servers respond by sending an IP address to the browser being used which allows the browser to locate the requested website. The syntax for a URL would be as follows:

- **Protocol Identifyer://FQDN/DirectoryName/specific-file or Program such as the following:**
  - HTTP://Cooltoys.com/westcoast/trains.html

The following is a brief explanation of the syntax used:
- **HTTP:** = Informs the operating system and browser what protocol is used for communication.
- **"//"** = Instructs an operating system to access a network device listed on the internet as "Cooltoys.com".
- **"/"** = Instructs an operating system to enter a directory called "westcoast".
- **"/trains.html"** = Instructs an operating system and browser to display a web document entitled "Trains.html".

Nodes, Clients, Identities and Character-Types:

Depending on which protocol or software is used on a network, devices can be identified many different ways. The following methods are ways in which network devices display their existence as well as what can be used for communications between devices (Note: Regardless of the naming convention, many characters are not compatible with many names such as "spaces" between characters and some special symbols such as " \ " or " * "):

- **Hostname** = Using Alpha-Numeric characters (A-Z and 0-9). Examples would be "PC_17", "Dad_Computer", "Room_012" etc. This type of name is totally arbitrary and can be changed. A simple view of a hostname can be displayed on Windows systems by typing in "hostname" and pressing "enter" when using a CLI.

- **IP Address (Decimal)** = Characters are numeric (0-9) and are arranged in four sections separated by decimals (.) called "Octets". In addition, the primary numbers used in IPv4 networks are between 0 and 255 in each section. Examples are "192.168.1.10" or "169.254.101.20". IP address arrangements appear in many network-related settings on computers, cell phones, televisions, etc. This type of identity can randomly change depending on how the network interface is configured. A simple view of an IP address can be displayed on Windows systems by typing in "ipconfig" and pressing "enter" when using a CLI.

- **Mac Address (Hexadecimal)** = Also called a "Physical Address" and uses a limited arrangement of Alpha-Numeric characters including only 0-9 and A-F (There are other hexadecimal character combinations but the ones listed are used in network technology). Usually arranged in three groups of four characters separated by decimals or six groups of two characters separated by hyphens (-). Examples would be A9-6F-CE-AA-87-99. The mac-address is actually encoded in the network interface of a device. It is globally unique and more like a network device's "fingerprint". This identity is configured to be permanent and can only be changed by persons with higher levels of electronics, programming or cyber-security experience. A view of a devices physical address can be displayed on Windows systems by typing in "ipconfig /all" and pressing "enter" when using a CLI.

- **Binary** = Binary characters are the foundation of computer and software technology. These characters are represented with either a "0" or a "1". Combinations of binary characters cause actions in software, hardware and identify devices. Often with programming, the two options for bits have specific meanings as in the following:
  - **0 = off, no or false.**
  - **1 = on, yes or true.**
  - Total numbers of combined characters have meaning in elements of instruction, storage and/or speed. Specific well-known combinations have the following names:
    - **Bit** = Single character as in "0" or "1".
    - **Nibble** = Four bits as in "0000" or "1111" or "0101".
    - **Byte (Sometimes called an "Octet")** = Eight bits, or two nibbles as in "11110000"

Chapter 5
Character Conversion Tables

Character Conversion Tables:

Many devices with one ID type must communicate with totally different device ID types. For this to occur, there is the need to convert between identities. For example, some situations require a binary identity to be displayed in decimal format. To understand this process, it is necessary to learn how to convert between the three following identities; decimal, binary and hexadecimal. A table which will be used a lot in this text is displayed below:

Network Related Numbers Conversion		
Decimal	Hexadecimal	Binary
0	0	0000
1	1	0001
2	2	0010
3	3	0011
4	4	0100
5	5	0101
6	6	0110
7	7	0111
8	8	1000
9	9	1001
10	A	1010
11	B	1011
12	C	1100
13	D	1101
14	E	1110
15	F	1111

There are many ways to convert numbers mathematically. When taking many certification examinations, calculators are not allowed and processing questions concerning math may result in a great loss of time (Most certification examinations have a specific time limit for completion). It is important to utilize a method which will render quicker results without the need for duplicated writing. In order to accomplish this goal, I (The writer) have created a "pointing table" which can expedite the process of number conversions as well as other related processes required in network technology and certifications. The writer has created a number of methods and tables which can assist the learning of conversions. One of the tables used is the "Decimal to Binary Conversions Table" displayed below:

Decimal to Binary Conversions							
128	64	32	16	8	4	2	1

- **Formula Legend:**
  1. **N1** = Original number.
  2. **R#** = Resultant number.

With the table above, it is possible to translate decimal numbers to binary and the reverse. No higher order math is necessary. Simply place numbers into the "value spaces" and either add or subtract depending on the desired operation. Using the table above, perform the following:

- **Convert the decimal number "3" into a binary value. Here is the overview:**
  1) Moving "left to right" indicate a binary "1" for any spot which can be subtracted from N1.
  2) Moving "left to right" indicate a binary "0" for any spot which cannot be subtracted from N1.
  3) When a number can be subtracted, do so and continue using the result (R#)

Let's work the problem:
- Step 1 = Left to right, find the value spot which can be SUBTRACTED FROM "3" (N1).
  1. The value spot "128" cannot be subtracted from "3".
     - ➢ Place a "0" in the binary row beneath the value spot.
     - ➢ Continue moving to the right.
  2. The value spot "64" cannot be subtracted from "3".
     - ➢ Place a "0" in the binary row beneath the value spot.
     - ➢ Continue moving to the right.
  3. The value spot "32" cannot be subtracted from "3".
     - ➢ Place a "0" in the binary row beneath the value spot.
     - ➢ Continue moving to the right.
  4. The value spot "16" cannot be subtracted from "3".
     - ➢ Place a "0" in the binary row beneath the value spot.
     - ➢ Continue moving to the right.
  5. The value spot "8" cannot be subtracted from "3".

➢ Place a "0" in the binary row. Continue moving to the right.

6. The value spot "4" cannot be subtracted from "3".
   ➢ Place a "0" in the binary row beneath the value spot.
   ➢ Continue moving to the right.

7. The value spot "2" CAN be subtracted from "3".
   ➢ Subtract the value spot (2) from the original number "3".
   ➢ We now using the remainder of "1" as the number we are evaluating.
      ❖ We call this "R1" (The digit changes based on what was left after subtracting the found number from N1).
   ➢ Place a "1" in the binary row beneath the value spot.
   ➢ Continue moving to the right.

8. The value spot "1" can be subtracted from "1" (R1).
   ➢ Subtract the number in the value spot (1) from the result number "1"
   ➢ We now using the remainder of "0" as the number we are evaluating.
      ❖ We call this "R2" (The digit changes based on changing resultants).
   ➢ Place a "1" in the binary row beneath the value spot. The results will look like table below:

Decimal to Binary Conversions							
128	64	32	16	8	4	2	1
0	0	0	0	0	0	1	1
X	X	X	X	X	X	(-2)	(0)

9. Going from left to right, add up all the value spot numbers which have a "1" beneath them (2 + 1 = 3).

10. The binary equivalent of the decimal number "3" = 00000011.
   ➢ Some books drop the zeros before the first 1 which makes the number display as "11". Don't be fooled. Always keep the zeros in mind!

Let's try another: Find the binary version of the decimal number 40. Remember the steps:

- Moving "left to right" indicate a binary "1" for any spot which can be subtracted from N1.
- Moving "left to right" indicate a binary "0" for any spot which cannot be subtracted from N1.
- When a number can be subtracted, do so and continue using the result (R#). In this case "N1" = "40"
    - Step 1 = Left to right, find the value spot which can be SUBTRACTED FROM "40" (N1).
        1. The value spot "128" cannot be subtracted from "40".
            - Place a "0" in the binary row beneath the value spot.
            - Continue moving to the right.
        2. The value spot "64" cannot be subtracted from "40".
            - Place a "0" in the binary row beneath the value spot.
            - Continue moving to the right.
        3. The value spot "32" CAN be subtracted from "40".
            - Subtract the number in the value spot (32) from the original number "40" (N1) leaving the first result of 8 (R1).
            - We are now using "8" as the number we are evaluating.
                - ❖ We call this "R1" (The digit changes based on changing resultants).
                - ❖ Continue moving to the right.
        4. The value spot "16" cannot be subtracted from "8".
            - Place a "0" in the binary row beneath the value spot.
            - Continue moving to the right.
        5. The value spot "8" CAN be subtracted from "8".
            - Subtract the number in the value spot (8) from the first result number "8" (R1) leaving the second result of 0 (R2).
            - We are now using "0" as the number we are evaluating.
                - ❖ We call this "R2" (The digit changes based on changing resultants).
            - Continue moving to the right.
        6. The value spot "4" cannot be subtracted from "0".
            - Place a "0" in the binary row beneath the value spot.
            - Continue moving to the right.
        7. The value spot "2" cannot be subtracted from "0".
            - Place a "0" in the binary row beneath the value spot.
            - Continue moving to the right.
        8. The value spot "2" cannot be subtracted from "0".

> Place a "0" in the binary row beneath the value spot.

9. Going from left to right, add up all the value spot numbers which have a "1" beneath them (32 + 8 = 4).

Decimal to Binary Conversions							
128	64	32	16	8	4	2	1
0	0	1	0	1	0	0	0
X	X	(-8)	X	(-0)	X	X	X

10. The binary equivalent of the decimal number "40" = 00101000.

> Some books drop the zeros before the first 1 which makes the number display as "101000". Don't be fooled. Always keep the zeros in mind.

Try a few of the numbers below on your own. Convert the following decimal numbers into binary:

1. 129 = Answer 10000001
2. 70 = Answer 01000110
3. 20 = Answer 00010100
4. 10 = Answer 00001010
5. 250 = Answer 11111010

Chapter 6
IP Addressing Versions and Concepts

IP Addressing Versions and Concepts:

Regardless of the type of software used or the type of network devices they all require identity information. We discussed the following identities in the section "Nodes, Clients and Identities". Different protocols use many different identities for communication but for our discussions we will primarily discuss "IP Addresses". The following areas will be the focus of the discussion of this book concerning IP addresses:

- **IP version 4** = One of the primary standards established by ARPANET for network identities on the internet. Although worldwide organizations formally established it in the mid-1980's, IPv4 routes much Internet traffic today and will more than likely exist for quite some time. Elements which allow IPv4's continued existence is in the elements that it is a widely used protocol in data communication and allows compatibility across a number of different network types. Multiple types of network devices support IPv4 and there are many features such as "Dynamic Host Configuration Protocol", "Vender Class" and many other utilities. IPv4 is a connectionless protocol which means that the source and destination does not have a dedicated connection but uses intermediary devices to transmit data in a "Relay-Race" fashion". It provides the logical connection between network devices by providing identification for each device. Due to this configuration, there is a possibility of failed delivery or even duplicated date being sent. Although the protocol has errors inherent in its composition, higher level protocols protect against errors. IPv4 uses a 32-bit (four-byte) method allowing for a total of 2^32 addresses (just over 4 billion addresses). The addresses are converted from binary to decimal when displayed for better understanding for humans. Because of the demand of the growing Internet, the available numbers of remaining addresses were nearing exhaustion anticipated between 2004 and 2011. The problem concerning "lack of available network addresses for the internet" was foreseen many years prior which gave rise to other methods of network addressing for the internet.
- **IP Version 6** = Internet Protocol version 6 (IPv6) is the version of the Internet Protocol (IP) initiated for use near the year 2011 which provides an identification for servers, routers and network devices system across the Internet. IPv6 was developed by the Internet Engineering Task Force (IETF) to address the foreseen exhaustion of available of IPv4 addresses. IPv6 uses a 128-bit address which provides for 2^28 which is a number so large it is said to be an "Undecillion". IPv6 addresses are

represented as eight groups of four "Hextets" or "Hexwords" separated by colons such as in the example; "2001:1234:abcd:9944:c6750:cf00:36bb:94ee". The example given in the previous sentence is called "uncompressed" although many times, the full address can be compressed by eliminating groups of zeros.

- **Classfull IP addressing** = Primary method used on the Internet from 1981 to about early 1990's. Using the Classfull method, address spaces are divided into five address classes of "A, B and C" with two more of "D" which is for "multicasting" and "E" reserved for military and experimental purposes. Below is an example of Classfull IP addressing:

Traditional Classfull IP Address Standards			
Class	Leading Octet	Subnet Mask	Maximum Hosts
A	0-126	255.0.0.0	16,777,214
B	127 - 191	255.255.0.0	65,534
C	192 - 223	255.255.255.0	254
D	224 - 239	Multicast	NA
E	240 - 247	Military Use	NA
*Note = This displays the maximum "Usable" hosts and not the pure mathematical derivatives.			

- **Classless IP Addressing** = Due to the growth of the internet, there was a need to extend the range of available addressing. IPv6 is a method but the primary restriction to it is that older IPv4 devices could not communicate using IPv6. A solution to the decreasing number of available IPv4 addresses was produced with the implementation of CIDR and VLSM:
  - **Classless Internet Domain Routing (CIDR)** = When networks were developed, traffic was routed based on matching Classfull IP Classes (i.e., "A, "B", "C", etc.) with a specific subnet mask ("255.0.0.0", "255.255.0.0" or "255.255.255.0"). Due to the increase in the number of devices, classfull IP addressing could not support the number of routes on the internet. IPv6 was created, but IPv4 will not understand routing from IPv6. Due to this challenge, programmers began to re-compile router and switch operating systems to utilize the "binary" form of numbers as opposed to the traditional method of "decimal" utilization. Because of this enhancement, subnet masks can include the following new octets: 128, 192, 224, 240, 248, 252, and 254. These new octets are combined with traditional IP addresses as in the examples below:

CIDR Examples	
Host IP	**Subnet Mask**
204.16.10.54	255.255.255.128
199.240.78.95	255.255.240.0
224.16.76.81	255.255.255.192

Netmask Conversions		
Binary	**Octet**	**CIDR**
10000000	128	/25
11000000	192	/26
11100000	224	/27
11110000	240	/28
11111000	248	/29
11111100	252	/30
11111110	254	/31
11111111	255	NA (Or /32)
Assumes 1st three octets of "255.255.255.x"		

> Although decimal numbers are displayed, the arrangement of the "Binary "0's" and "1's" dictate network parameters such as:
>   ❖ Number of networks
>   ❖ Number of hosts
>   ❖ Paths between networks
> **Variable Length Subnet Masks (VLSM)** = Paralleling the utilization of CIDR, the method of documenting IP configurations has also evolved. As opposed to using decimal numbers, the amount of "1's" in "binary" are added up and a decimal number is used to reflect the total written at the end of an IP address after a "/" character (Often called a "forward slash"). Take the following for example:
>   ❖ Traditional subnet mask = 255.255.255.128
>   1) Binary format
>   11111111.11111111.11111111.10000000
>   2) Count number of binary "1's" = 8+8+8+1 = 25 total.

3) VLSM documentation = /25
- o **Reserved Addresses** = When using IPv4, IPv6 or CIDR, specific types of IP addresses have special uses. We often call these addresses "Reserved" or "Special Use". Regardless of their use, they both have one common element. Reserved IP addresses are not to be used on devices directly connected to the internet (On the Department of Defense backbone). If reserved IP addresses are used on devices which are directly connected to the internet backbone, the situation will result in the device not communication or a conflict with other devices on the internet. The following are some of the "reserved" addresses:
  - ➤ **169.254.X.Y** = Network systems will self-assign an address within in this range if a DHCP server cannot be contacted.
  - ➤ **192.168.X.Y** = Often used for private networks or training purposes.
  - ➤ **127.0.0.1** = This is called the "loopback" and "localhost" address. This address is used as a utility to ascertain if a network devices interface can be contacted by the rest of the network. The loopback is often used if the network devices IP address is hidden. Using a "ping" command, a technician can perform the following to test if the network device he or she is working on can be contacted by other devices.
  - ➤ Some other reserved IP address appear in the chart below:

Reserved/Special Use IP Addresses
10.0.0.0 – 10.255.255.255
172.16.0.0 – 172.31.255.255
192.168.0.0 – 192.168.255.255
127.0.0.1 - 127.255.255.254

Parts of an IP Address:

Based on the communication requirements on a network, various methods of node identification can be used (As in the prior mentioned methods of "hostname", "physical address" and/or "IP address", etc.). When using IP addresses, specific sections of an address have terms which are used to describe their purpose.

- **Network Address/ID** = The section of an IP address which all nodes on a section of a network have in common. Often times, it is the leading numbers on an IP address leading from left to right. An example would be 209.15.X.Y subnet mask of 255.255.0.0. The first two octets identify the network address (Traditionally, the section of the subnet mask will give an idea of the network address because whichever octet section used by the network address ID will reflect the same number of "255's" in the subnet mask.
    - o Think of it like a "last name" on a family. There could be multiple people in a family. Such as the "Smith" family. All of the people in the family could be referred to as "the Smith" family. A network or network section uses the network address and it is common on all computers such as in the "Branch Office" network.
- **Host ID/node ID** = Section of an IP address which is unique for individual systems. This would be like the "first name" of all the people in the "Smith" family. There could be "Bob Smith", "Sam Smith" and "Sally Smith". In reference to a network, think of the following computers:
    - o 172.16.10.10 = Part of the "172.16.10" network but the host ID is "10".
    - o 172.16.10.15 = Part of the "172.16.10" network but the host ID is "15".
    - o 172.16.10.20 = Part of the "172.16.10" network but the host ID is "20".

When there are subnets which need to function with other subnets, somewhere on the network there must exist a routing device of some type. Before discussion and attempting labs in subnetting, the following is a brief review about IP types:

- **Classfull IP addressing** = Primary method used on the Internet from 1981 to about early 1990's. Using the Classfull method, address spaces are divided into five address classes of "A, B and C" with two more such as "D" which is for "multicasting" and "E" reserved for military and experimental purposes. Below is an example of Classfull IP addressing:

Traditional Classfull IP Address Standards			
Class	**Leading Octet**	**Subnet Mask**	**Maximum Hosts**
A	0-126	255.0.0.0	16,777,214
B	127 - 191	255.255.0.0	65,534
C	192 - 223	255.255.255.0	254
D	224 - 239	Multicast	NA
E	240 - 247	Military Use	NA
*Note = This displays the maximum "Usable" hosts and not the pure mathematical derivatives.			

- **Classless IP Addressing** = Due to the growth of the internet, there was a need to extend the range of available addressing. IPv6 is a method but the primary restriction to it is that older IPv4 devices could not communicate using IPv6. A solution to the decreasing number of available IPv4 addresses was produced with the implementation of VLSM and CIDR.
  - **Classless Internet Domain Routing (CIDR)** = When networks were developed, traffic was routed based on matching Classes (i.e., "A, "B", "C", etc.) with a specific subnet mask ("255.0.0.0", "255.255.0.0" or "255.255.255.0"). Due to the increase in the number of devices, classfull IP addressing could not support the number of routes on the internet. IPv6 was created, but IPv4 will not understand routing from IPv6. Due to this challenge, programmers began to re-compile router operating systems in a manner which utilizes the "binary" form of numbers as opposed to the traditional method of "decimal" utilization. Because of this enhancement, subnet mask octets can include the following 9 numbers: 0, 128, 192, 224, 240, 248, 252, 254 and 255. With this method, the arrangement of "0's" or "1's" which are the "Binary" version of the decimal numbers dictate the following:
    - ☐ **Number of Networks**
    - ☐ **Number of Hosts**
    - ☐ **Routing Paths**
  - **Variable Length Subnet Masks (VLSM)** = Paralleling the utilization of CIDR, the method of documenting IP configurations has also evolved. Utilizing terms such as "Class A, B or C" or the traditional subnet masks such as "255.0.0.0, 255.255.0.0 and 255.255.255.0" are often replaced with the following class "C" CIDR examples:

Netmask Conversions		
Binary	**Octet**	**CIDR**
10000000	128	/25
11000000	192	/26
11100000	224	/27
11110000	240	/28
11111000	248	/29
11111100	252	/30
11111110	254	/31
11111111	255	NA (Or /32)
Assumes 1st three octets of "255.255.255.x"		

- o As opposed to using decimal numbers as the subnet mask, the total amount of "binary" 1's" in the subnet mask are added together and a two-character decimal number is used to reflect the subnet mask after the IP address and a "/" character (Often called a "forward slash"). Take the following for example:
  - ☐ Given CIDR subnet mask = 255.255.255.128
    - ➢ Binary format 11111111.11111111.11111111.00000000
    - ➢ Count number of binary "1's" = 8+8+8+1 = 25 total.
    - ➢ VLSM documentation = /25

IP version 6 Format and Structure:

The display of an IP version 6 address uses what is known as "hexadecimal" characters. These characters include the alpha-numeric values of "A, B, C, D, E, F" and "0, 1, 2, 3, 4, 5, 6, 8 and 9". Remember that any character viewed in a character format is only for the human eye. Computers actually use the "binary" equivalent any displayed character. Below are the listed hexadecimal characters associated with their binary equivalence:

Network Related Numbers Conversion		
Decimal	Hexadecimal	Binary
0	0	0000
1	1	0001
2	2	0010
3	3	0011
4	4	0100
5	5	0101
6	6	0110
7	7	0111
8	8	1000
9	9	1001
10	A	1010
11	B	1011
12	C	1100
13	D	1101
14	E	1110
15	F	1111

Let's look at the various formats and displays of the IPv6 format and characters. IPv6 addresses are written as a string of hexadecimal values. Take the following for example: 2001:1234:EF00:5678:9AAC:DDEE:FF11:ABCD

- Written in full form displays 32 hexadecimal characters.
  - o Every 4 bits = Single hexadecimal character.
- Total bits length is 128.
  - o Display is separated into eight sections separated by colons.
    - ◻ Example as in = $x^1:x^2:x^3:x^4:x^5:x^6:x^7:x^8$.
    - ◻ Each "x" = 16 bits in or four hexadecimal characters often called "Hextet" or "Hexword"

IPv6 Hexadecimal Address to Binary Conversions:

The following are some examples of how to read and convert the sections of a IPv6 IP address. We will keep it simple by using what is known as a "broadcast IPv6 Address which reads as "FFFF:FFFF:FFFF:FFFF:FFFF:FFFF:FFFF:FFFF". You will notice that there are 8 sections which are separated by colons (:). Each of those sections is actually 16 binary "ones (1)". If the same address was displayed in binary, it would look like the following (For ease viewing, the 8 sections are separated into different colors.):

11111111111111111111111111111111111111111111111111111**1111111111111111**
11111111111111111111111111111111111**111111111111111111111111111111111111**

Counting all the bits from left to right, you notice that there are a total of 128-bits. When the bits are converted into hexadecimal, colons separate (:) every 16 bits creating 8 sections called "hextets" or "hexwords" as in "FFFF:FFFF:FFFF:FFFF:FFFF:FFFF:FFFF:FFFF". Each character (Not including the colons) represent the value of 4 binary characters. In the example we are using, each "F" is actually 4 binary "ones", as hexadecimal "F" = Binary "1111" and "Hexadecimal "FF" = binary "11111111". Let's take the explanation even further with the following examples:

- Hex FFFF = Binary of 1111111111111111
- Hex 0000 = Binary of 0000000000000000
- Hex D4DB = Binary of 1101010011011011

Ipv6 Address Sections:

When using IPv6 it is required to understand the different sections included in the 128-bit identity. Similar to IPv4 sections which include a network section/ID, host section/ID and netmask indicator, IPv6 addresses have sections which provide similar functions but use different names. The following are the sections for IPv6:

- **Prefix** = Often times, internet service providers supply available IPv6 public addresses with the first 64 bits representing the entire network (Often indicated by "/64" appearing after the IP address). This requires every system on that network to have an identical collection of bits moving from the "Left-to-Right".
  - Utilizes the bits moving from "Left-to-Right" (Often called the "Leftmost Bits").
  - Devices on the same network will have a matching arrangement of "0's" and "1's" on the leftmost side.
  - Expressed with a "/" similar to CIDR.
  - Comparable to an IPv4 subnet mask.
  - Examples of 4 systems in the same network would be as follows:
    - 2001:0db8: fd30:7654:1085:0099:fecc:5871 /64
    - 2001:0db8: fd30:7654:abcd:0052:e433:0001 /64
    - 2001:0db8: fd30:7654:dea0:8766:d222:98cc /64
    - 2001:0db8: fd30:7654:76ff:0433:5432:bb98 /64

☐ The "/64" indicates that 1st 64 bits moving from "left-to-right" on all the nodes are identical.

- **Interface ID** = On a flat network, this will be the last 64bits of the IP address after the Prefix section. This section is used for the unique identifier of the specific node. Below, the section highlighted in "BOLD BLACK" would represent the interface ID. Examples of 4 systems in the same network would be as follows:
  - 2001:0db8:fd30:7654:1085:0099:fecc:5871 /64
  - 2001:0db8:fd30:7654:abcd:0052:e433:0001 /64
  - 2001:0db8:fd30:7654:dea0:8766:d222:98cc /64
  - 2001:0db8:fd30:7654:76ff:0433:5432:bb98 /64

IP v6 written format methods:

Preferred Format = IPv6 addresses are very long in written format. This is what is called the "Preferred Format" which requires the display of all 32 hexadecimal characters. Below are examples of this format:

- 2001:0db8:0000:0000:0000:0578:abcd:00cb
- 2001:0000:abcd:0cbd:0000:321c:951d:fe35
- Fe80:1700:0000:00ce:0000:0000:0000:567d

Compressed Format = There are two options however which can be used to reduce the written/displayed characters of the IP address although all 128 bits are still being utilized. This method is referred to as "Compressed Format". The two methods are as follows:

- **Method #1** = Any leading hexadecimal 0's (zeros) in any 16-bit section (hextet) can be omitted:
- **Method #2** = Any string of one or more hexadecimal 0's (zeros) in a complete 16-bit segments (hextets) can be replace with a zero (0) between colons or simply a double colon (::).
  - The double colon (::) can only be used once within an address.
  - This is commonly known as "Compressed Format".

Let's evaluate the method #1 which allows any leading hexadecimal zeros ("0's") in any 16-bit section (hextet) to be omitted. Using a single hextet example, notice how the method can be implemented:

- "01AB" can be written as "1AB"
- "09F0" can be written as "9F0"
- "0A00" can be written as "A00"

- "0000" can be written as ":0:"

Below are full text examples using the leading zero removal method:

Example 1:
- Preferred Format = 2001:0db8:0000:0000:0000:0578:abcd:00cb
- Preceding Zero Removal Format = 2001:db8:0000:0000:0000:578:abcd:cb

Example 1:
- Preferred Format = 2001:0000:00cd:0cbd:0000:021c:951d:0035
- Preceding Zero Removal Format = 2001:0000:cd:cbd:0000:21c:951d:35

Let's evaluate the method #2 which allows any string of one or more 16-bit segments (hextets) consisting of all 0's to be replaced with a zero between colons (:0:) or simply a double colon (::).
- Note: The double colon (::) can only be used once within an address.
- This is commonly known as "Compressed Format".
- Using a four hextet example, notice how the method can be implemented:
  - **"FE80:0000:0000:CD00"** can be written as **"FE80::CD00"**
  - **"FE80:1234:0000:0000"** can be written as **"FE80:1234:0:"**
  - **"FE80:0000:0000:0000"** can be written as **"FE80::"**

Below are additional examples using the Compression Method (Note, the syntax ": :" and can only be used once in a given IP address):

- Preferred Format = 2001:0db8:0000:0000:0000:0578:abcd:00cb
  - Compressed Format = 2001:0db8:0:0:0:0578:abcd:00cb
  - Or: 2001:0db8: :0578:abcd:00cb

- Preferred Format = 2001:0000:abcd:0cbd:0000:321c:951d:fe35
  - Compressed Format = 2001: :abcd:0cbd:0:321c:951d:fe35

- Preferred Format = Fe80:1700:0000:00ce:0000:0000:0000:567d
  - Compressed Format = Fe80:1700: :00ce:0:567d

Reserved IPv6 addresses:

In IPv4, a number of IP addresses are classified as "Reserved" or "Special Use". A fast review of the following are examples:
- 169.254.x.y = Automatic Private IP Addressing.
- 127.0.0.1 = Local Host or Loopback Address

- 192.168.1.y = Internal private for testing and home networks.

IPv6 also has versions of IP addresses which provide similar functions although they have different names. Below are some of the special use IP addresses in IPv6. They are also matched with IPv4 types for easy comparison:

- **::/128 (Unspecified address)** = Indicates that the node does not have an IP address at present.
    o   Similar to "0.0.0.0" from IPv4.
- **::1/128 (Loopback)** = Used to test the configuration of TCP/IP on the local host.
    o   Similar to "127.0.0.1" from IPv4.

- **FC00::/ (Unique local)** = Local addressing within a site or between a limited number of sites.
    o   Similar to private IP addresses such as "172.16.x.y" and "192.168.x.y" from IPv4.

- **FE80:: (Link-local)** = Used to communicate with other devices on the same local network. Means that system has assigned itself an IP address
    o   Similar to "169.254.x.y" and APIPA from IPv4.

- **2001:: (Global unicast)** = Internet routable addresses accessible on the internet.
    o   This is the global unicast network prefix.
    o   Similar to a public IPv4 address.
    o   Static or dynamic.

- **FF00:(Multicast)** = Equivalent to the IPv4 224.x.x.x Class "D" addresses.

How DHCP Allocates Addresses (In Brief):

Often times, there are hundreds of computers which require addresses on a network. Not only is it an immense task to manually configure each computer, but there is a great possibility that duplicate addresses will be applied to multiple computers which can hamper and even disable entire networks. Due to this requirement of networks, there are methods in which clients can receive an address from a network device normally called a "DHCP" or "BOOTP" server. DHCP is an abbreviation for "Dynamic Host Configuration Protocol." "BOOTP" is an older method of tracking and distributing addresses and will not be illustrated in this text. A DHCP device or "Server" can be an operating system on a computer or simply a device which performs the addressing function. For our discussion, we will concentrate on the DHCP Server function implemented in Windows Server Networks as they relate to network clients.

On most computer networks, when clients are turned on, they have no IP address settings. During their boot-up, they will advertise their existence with what is called a "Broadcast" which is a "Scream to the Network" that the device would like an IP address given to it. The broadcast is associated with the "physical" or "MAC" address of the device (i.e., "3D-44-AC-FC-55-66"). Often the "broadcast" address appears in the following forms (In IPv4 and Hexadecimal):

- "0.0.0.0"
- "255.255.255.255"
- "FF-FF-FF-FF-FF-FF"

The signal is "heard" by a "DHCP" server which in turn, sends an IP address to the client by using the "physical" address as the target. Once the client agrees to use the offered IP address, the DHCP server records the address as given out and will not use it again until the client no longer requires the address, such as when the computer is turned off. The default time that is often set on Windows clients is about 8 days, but this time can be shortened or lengthened. In addition to an IP address, the client is also given the following network settings (May be more or less depending on the network):
- **Subnet Mask**
- **Domain Name**
- **Default Gateway location.**
- **Domain Name Server location.**

Oftentimes, a device will fail at receiving an IP address for a multitude of reasons. Using CLI commands, it is possible to ascertain if a network device was unsuccessful in IP attainment. Using the normal utility "ipconfig", if the address appears with the first two octets of "169.254.x.y" and a subnet mask of "255.255.0.0" the following is assumed:

- **The computer is connected to a network.**
- **Electronically, the network card interface and all associated cables are connected.**

- **The client was not able to receive an address from a DHCP server.**

The ip address of "169.254.x.y" is defined as "APIPA" (Automatic Private IP Addressing). This is the result of the process of a network device giving itself an IP address due to inability to communicate with a DHCP server. Prior to assigning itself an IP address, the client will use "ICMP" (Internet Control Messaging Protocol) to "Ping" an IP address it desires to use in the "169.254.x.y" range. If no other device responds, the client will use the address. "Ping" is a CLI network utility often used in network troubleshooting. The command will display if a specific network device has the ability to be contacted. The format to use the command is as follows:

- **Ping <ip address of target network device>**

Below is a display of a ping when a device is successfully contacted. Depending on the operating systems, successful detection of a network device will render 3 to 8 "positive replies:

```
Command Prompt

Microsoft Windows [Version 10.0.14393]
(c) 2016 Microsoft Corporation. All rights reserved.

C:\Users\c308>ping 10.10.41.76

Pinging 10.10.41.76 with 32 bytes of data:
Reply from 10.10.41.76: bytes=32 time<1ms TTL=128
Reply from 10.10.41.76: bytes=32 time<1ms TTL=128
Reply from 10.10.41.76: bytes=32 time<1ms TTL=128
Reply from 10.10.41.76: bytes=32 time<1ms TTL=128

Ping statistics for 10.10.41.76:
    Packets: Sent = 4, Received = 4, Lost = 0 (0% loss),
Approximate round trip times in milli-seconds:
    Minimum = 0ms, Maximum = 0ms, Average = 0ms
```

If a device is not located, the following on the next page would be the response:

```
C:\ C:\WINDOWS\system32\cmd.exe

C:\>ping 57.32.54.99

Pinging 57.32.54.99 with 32 bytes of data:

Request timed out.
Request timed out.
Request timed out.
Request timed out.

Ping statistics for 57.32.54.99:
    Packets: Sent = 4, Received = 0, Lost = 4 (100% loss),

C:\>
```

Many times, network technicians require more than 3 to 8 responses regardless of if they are positive or negative. In this situation, a "switch" to the "ping" option is utilized which will cause the ping to continue until manually terminated (Often called an "extended" or "infinite" ping). To terminate an extended ping, the control key combination "Ctrl+C" must be performed. The format and an illustration are as follows:

```
C:\ C:\WINDOWS\system32\cmd.exe

C:\>ping 98.139.180.149 -t

Pinging 98.139.180.149 with 32 bytes of data:

Reply from 98.139.180.149: bytes=32 time=34ms TTL=50
Reply from 98.139.180.149: bytes=32 time=46ms TTL=50
Reply from 98.139.180.149: bytes=32 time=34ms TTL=50
Reply from 98.139.180.149: bytes=32 time=51ms TTL=50
Reply from 98.139.180.149: bytes=32 time=46ms TTL=50
Reply from 98.139.180.149: bytes=32 time=26ms TTL=50
Reply from 98.139.180.149: bytes=32 time=21ms TTL=50
Reply from 98.139.180.149: bytes=32 time=26ms TTL=50
Reply from 98.139.180.149: bytes=32 time=33ms TTL=50
Reply from 98.139.180.149: bytes=32 time=24ms TTL=50

Ping statistics for 98.139.180.149:
    Packets: Sent = 10, Received = 10, Lost = 0 (0% loss),
Approximate round trip times in milli-seconds:
    Minimum = 21ms, Maximum = 51ms, Average = 34ms
Control-C
^C
C:\>_
```

Manually Configure an IP Address on Windows Systems:

Depending on the device or operating system, in order to communicate with other network devices there is the requirement for settings which allow transmission and reception of signals. In order for this to occur, devices have to share methods of communications commonly referred to as protocols. There are multiple protocols used in present network technology. The discussions in this text will primarily revolve around the protocol classified as TCP/IP (Transmission Control Protocol/Internet Protocol). This method of communication has two versions utilized presently of "v4" and "v6". Much of our discussion will relate to version 4. In addition, many of the sections discussed will be directly related to Microsoft Operating Systems as well as the Cisco IOS.

When utilizing Windows operating systems in network environments, there are both GUI and CLI methods of viewing and manipulating network configurations. When using CLI, the command prompt is activated and then we will use the command IPCONFIG. When using this command in its smallest format, the CLI displays basic network settings.

```
C:\WINDOWS\system32\cmd.exe                                      _ □ ×

C:\>ipconfig

Windows IP Configuration

Ethernet adapter Local Area Connection 3:

        Media State . . . . . . . . . . . : Media disconnected
Ethernet adapter Local Area Connection 5:

        Media State . . . . . . . . . . . : Media disconnected
Ethernet adapter Wireless Network Connection 6:

        Connection-specific DNS Suffix  . :
        IP Address. . . . . . . . . . . . : 192.168.1.152
        Subnet Mask . . . . . . . . . . . : 255.255.255.0
        Default Gateway . . . . . . . . . : 192.168.1.1

C:\>
```

When performing the basic command of IPCONFIG the following are explanations of the display:
- **IP Address** = Decimal identity of computer on a TCP/IP network.
- **Subnet Mask** = Provides segmentation of groups of computers.
- **Default-Gateway** = Point which allows a section of a network to communicate with devices outside of that network.

The command also has optional modifications available which will show more specific displays of network configurations or allow the use of advanced features and tasks. In order to use the enhanced features,.. additional words and characters must be appended to the command. The character which must be added is often called a "Forward Slash" or a "Switch" normally represented by using "/". The "Switch" is followed by a number of other commands which can perform a number of operations. The most common enhanced command is by adding the "All" parameter. This command will display a complete readout of all the settings presently used by the windows client as follows:

```
C:\WINDOWS\system32\cmd.exe                                    _ □

C:\>ipconfig /all

Windows IP Configuration

        Host Name . . . . . . . . . . . . : 3Com
        Primary Dns Suffix  . . . . . . . :
        Node Type . . . . . . . . . . . . : Hybrid
        IP Routing Enabled. . . . . . . . : No
        WINS Proxy Enabled. . . . . . . . : No
        DNS Suffix Search List. . . . . . : router.home

Ethernet adapter Local Area Connection 3:

        Media State . . . . . . . . . . . : Media disconnected
        Description . . . . . . . . . . . : Realtek PCIe GBE Family Controller
        Physical Address. . . . . . . . . : 40-09-4F-06-09-DD

Ethernet adapter Local Area Connection 5:

        Media State . . . . . . . . . . . : Media disconnected
        Description . . . . . . . . . . . : 3Com EtherLink XL 10/100 PCI For Com
plete PC Management NIC (3C905C-TX) #4
        Physical Address. . . . . . . . . : 00-09-4F-5F-DD-09-4F

Ethernet adapter Wireless Network Connection 6:

        Connection-specific DNS Suffix  . : router.home
        Description . . . . . . . . . . . : Belkin USB Adaptor
        Physical Address. . . . . . . . . : EC-09-4F-B0-B6-DD
        Dhcp Enabled. . . . . . . . . . . : Yes
        Autoconfiguration Enabled . . . . : Yes
        IP Address. . . . . . . . . . . . : 192.168.1.152
        Subnet Mask . . . . . . . . . . . : 255.255.255.0
        Default Gateway . . . . . . . . . : 192.168.1.1
        DHCP Server . . . . . . . . . . . : 192.168.1.1
        DNS Servers . . . . . . . . . . . : 192.168.1.1
        Lease Obtained. . . . . . . . . . : Saturday, August 12, 2007 7:40:59 AM

        Lease Expires . . . . . . . . . . : Sunday, August 13, 2007 7:40:59 AM

C:\>_
```

IP addresses are essential in network communications on TCP/IP networks. There are a number of methods utilized to establish address settings on network devices. The following are some of the options:

- **Static Address (Manual)** = This allows an IP address to be established by a technician. The technician can either use a CLI or GUI to manually type in an IP address. To set an IP address using CLI, the following could be done:
  - **netsh interface ipv4 set address name="3Com19111" static 100.100.100.10 255.255.255.0 100.100.100.100**

The above command inserted "100.100.100.10" as the computer's IP address with a subnet mask of 255.255.255.0 and a default-gateway setting of 100.100.100.100. To set an IP address using the GUI, the following would be performed:

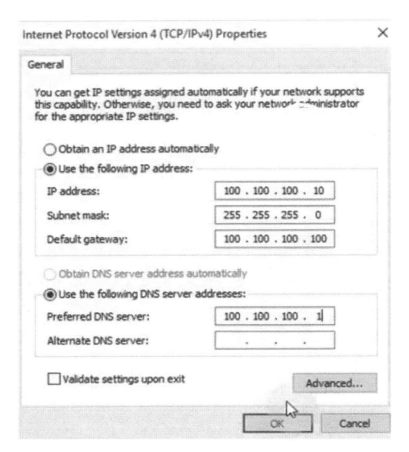

Chapter 7
Software Communications
Ports/Sockets

Software Communications Ports/Sockets:

Earlier in this book, there is the mention of "protocols" which are simply "rules of communication" between network devices. Some of the protocols listed were "DHCP", "Telnet" and "HTTP". As long as network devices are using similar protocols, they will have the ability to communicate and/or exchange data. There are other elements related to network communications, however. These other elements are classified as "Ports".

"Port" is a term used to identify a logical, software path between devices. Whatever media (Cable, wireless, etc.) software uses to travel is not a single cable in function. In actuality, there are 65,535 different paths of communications available between any devices communicating on a network. The following diagram is an example using "DHCP", "HTTP" and "Telnet":

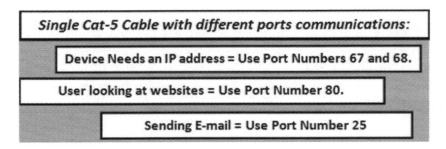

Single Cat-5 Cable with different ports communications:

Device Needs an IP address = Use Port Numbers 67 and 68.

User looking at websites = Use Port Number 80.

Sending E-mail = Use Port Number 25

Any or all of these ports can be used at any given time. Different types of software are configured to communicate on different ports. The picture below displays different communications occurring on a computer which is presently viewing "Disney.com". The command used in the command line interface (CLI) after visiting the website is "netstat –a". There are a number of ports which display "Disney.com" related entries. Each of the entries which reflect "website" communications will display as an IP address with a "colon (:)" followed with "HTTP" and "HTTPS":

```
TCP   192.168.1.118:63508   server-54-192-36-235:http   LAST_ACK
TCP   192.168.1.118:63510   ec2-54-243-80-169:http   LAST_ACK
TCP   192.168.1.118:63511   server-54-192-36-125:http   LAST_ACK
TCP   192.168.1.118:63512   server-54-192-36-125:http   LAST_ACK
TCP   192.168.1.118:63513   server-54-192-36-125:http   LAST_ACK
TCP   192.168.1.118:63521   server-54-192-36-125:http   LAST_ACK
TCP   192.168.1.118:63527   server-54-192-36-235:http   LAST_ACK
TCP   192.168.1.118:63537   133:http                    LAST_ACK
TCP   192.168.1.118:63539   192.229.210.12:http         LAST_ACK
TCP   192.168.1.118:63540   ec2-52-27-8-169:http        TIME_WAIT
TCP   192.168.1.118:63541   ec2-184-73-198-200:http     TIME_WAIT
TCP   192.168.1.118:63545   ec2-52-205-153-11:http      TIME_WAIT
TCP   192.168.1.118:63546   ec2-54-88-194-5:https       ESTABLISHED
TCP   192.168.1.118:63547   192.229.210.12:http         LAST_ACK
TCP   192.168.1.118:63548   192.229.210.12:http         LAST_ACK
TCP   192.168.1.118:63550   ec2-54-88-194-5:http        TIME_WAIT
TCP   192.168.1.118:63552   a184-26-44-105:http         LAST_ACK
```

The Department of Defense (DOD) along with other agencies (i.e., InterNIC) support standard documentation to categorize which ports are used for specific communications. Many vendors have accepted agreements to create software for similar purposes to all communicate on the same port (i.e., web browser creators such as "Firefox", "Chrome" and "Internet Explorer" all use ports 90 and 443 for default website viewing). Other ports are also standardized for other uses which may periodically move to other ports. Since there are 65,535 ports, many are not identified for any particular use. Any port can be utilized at any time for any transmission type without any updates to any international standard documents. Due to the different elements involved in the use of different ports, there are terms which are used to describe the port categories along with their respective numbers as in the following:

Port Range	Category
1-1023	Well-known
1024-49151	Registered
49152-65535	Dynamic

Although specific ports are associated with a particular function or software, it is possible to reconfigure software to utilize other ports. For example, "Telnet" uses port 23 while e-mail (SMTP) uses port 25. It is possible to configure telnet to test an e-mail server by making telnet use port 25. The process for testing an e-mail server is beyond the scope of this book, but it required mention for those who desire network certification. Often time on certification examinations, it is required to identify some specific ports and protocols within the "Well-known (Also called "Commonly Used")" or commonly used range. The table below displays many of the ports often manipulated in troubleshooting and or normally assessed on certification examinations:

Port	Protocol
20, 21	File Transfer Protocol (FTP)
23	Telnet
25	Simple Mail Transfer Protocol (SMTP)
53	Domain Name Server (DNS)
67, 68	Dynamic Host Configuration Protocol (DHCP)
69	Trivial File Transfer Protocol (TFTP)
80	HyperText Transfer Protocol (HTTP)
110	Post Office Protocol (POP3)
143	Internet Message Access Protocol (IMAP4)
443	HTTP with Secure Sockets Layer (SSL)
3389	Remote Desktop (RDP)

Chapter 8
What is a "MAC Address"?

What is a "MAC Address?

When working in the field of network technology it is required to understand at least three identities which network devices can use to identify themselves and to be contacted. Those identities are as follows:

- **Hostname** = Appears as a simple word such as "PC1" or "MyComputer".
- **IP address** = Decimal Identity such as "172.16.20.1"
- **MAC Address** = Combination of letters and decimal numbers such as "A8-45-CD-23-FA-BE"

In our present discussion, we will evaluate "MAC Addresses". MAC (Often stands for "Media Access Control") Address. This identity is one the most essential of network device identities. Many people compare the Mac Address to a human "finger print". This collection of letters and numbers are globally unique. Essentially, this means that there should be no duplicated Mac address on any network device in the world when the device is produced by a manufacture. A Mac address is programmed into a ROM chip that is part of the network devices' "network interface (NIC)". If the NIC is ever moved to another network device (i.e., "Out of one computer and inserted into another") the MAC will follow the NIC and now be part of the network device of which it is inserted.

Because the code for the MAC is part of a piece of hardware, we often refer to it as a "Physical Address". In order to view a computers MAC you would utilize the command "IPCONFIG /ALL" such as in the following example:

```
C:\WINDOWS\system32\cmd.exe                                        - □

          Description . . . . . . . . . . . . : 3Com EtherLink XL 10/100 PCI For Com
plete PC Management NIC (3C905C-TX) #4
          Physical Address. . . . . . . . . : 00-50-DA-5F-77-0C

Ethernet adapter Wireless Network Connection 6:

          Connection-specific DNS Suffix  . :
          Description . . . . . . . . . . :
          Physical Address. . . . . . . . . : │EC-1A-59-B0-B6-DD│
          Dhcp Enabled. . . . . . . . . . . : Yes
          Autoconfiguration Enabled . . . . : Yes
          IP Address. . . . . . . . . . . . : 192.168.1.152
          Subnet Mask . . . . . . . . . . . : 255.255.255.0
          Default Gateway . . . . . . . . . : 192.168.1.1
          DHCP Server . . . . . . . . . . . : 192.168.1.1
          DNS Servers . . . . . . . . . . . : 192.168.1.1
          Lease Obtained. . . . . . . . . . :
          Lease Expires . . . . . . . . . . :

C:\>
```

When network devices communicate, although IP addresses are configured, most communications occur using the MAC address of the computer. This is because the MAC address is more dependable. The other two identities on network devices (i.e., "Hostname" and "ip address") can be easily changed. MAC addresses do not change (Except when a computer uses a "flash update" for repairs or participates in "Spoofing" to attempt to compromise a network). MAC addresses are a total of 12 characters normally separated into groups of two such as the following:

- **CC:CC:CC:MM:MM:MM**
- **CC-CC-CC-MM-MM-MM**

When initial communications occur between servers and other network devices, particularly inside a specific LAN, the IP addresses between nodes are used. After a successful communication of some sort occurs,.the devices exchange MAC addresses. This allows faster and more stable communications due to a table being used called "ARP (Address Resolution Protocol). The ARP table is created as successful communications are established between computers. To witness the processes of network devices using ARP and MAC addresses for communication, the following utilities can be used:

- **Arp –a** = This command shows all the IP addresses and MAC associations known by a computer. Some may be "dynamic" (Subject to change) while others will be "Static (Will not change)"
- **Arp –d *** = This command clears all IP address to MAC associations.
- **Nbtstat –w.x.y.z** = Command will display all identities associated with an IP address in the Arp Table.

How to Convert "MAC Address" to "Binary"

The characters include both reading letters and decimal numbers limited to "0 thru 9" and "A – F". Computers cannot process double-characters such as the number "13" or "10". In order to process double digit numbers for network technology (Or numbers higher than the decimal number "9") a letter was selected to represent certain numbers which have two digits. The following table show the numbers which are represented by each hexadecimal character:

Hex	Represents		
1	1		
2	2		
3	3		
4	4	A	10
5	5	B	11
6	6	C	12
7	7	D	13
8	8	E	14
9	9	F	15

Remember, computers only show letter and number characters so humans can understand the message. Computers and other network devices have to use binary numbers. With hexadecimal numbers, each character is actually a representation of a collection of binary characters ("0's" or "1's"). Each character always represents four "bits" **(Called a "Nibble"). Understanding that a MAC has 12 hexadecimal characters, multiplying each character by "four bits" will render a total number of 128 bits**. These bits are what are used by computer hardware and software for functions. The hexadecimal readout is only so humans can better differentiate between different MACS. In the field of network technology, it is necessary to understand how binary collections create specific MAC addresses. To provide this function the following "Hex to Binary" table is used:

Hex to Binary Conversions								
A	8	4	2	1	8	4	2	1
B								
C								

Notice that the table is similar to the "Decimal to Binary" scale in which it has eight "value spaces" and it has three levels. The following are the functions of each level:

- **A-Level (Value Areas)** = Indicates 8,4,2,1-8,4,2,1
- **B-Level (Yes/No Area)** = Indicates if can be subtracted from hexadecimal character.
- **C-Level (Hex Character)** = Specific character being evaluated.

Using the table,..it is possible to convert between hexadecimal characters and their associated "nibbles" or binary equivalence. Using the table and a process, we can carry out the conversion using the following the steps:
1. Locate a full 12-character MAC address.
2. Isolate the first set of Hex characters (Separated by " : " or " . ").
3. Locate the "Left-most" hex character in and place in "C=Left" of the conversion table.
4. Locate the "Right-most" hex character in and place in "C=Right" of the conversion table.
5. Subtract all "A-Row" numbers from the "C-Row" numbers from left to right.
6. All numbers you cannot subtract, record as a binary "0" in the "B-Row".
7. All numbers you can subtract, record as a binary "1" in the B-Row and retain remainder for next subtraction.
8. Continue until you have two complete "Nibbles" on the "B-Row".

Take the following example: Given the MAC address of 23-3C-DD-AB-FE-72, what is the binary version of the 2nd character set? Let's work the problem:
- 2nd character set = "3C"
- Place the characters on the conversion chart as in the following (Remember to convert "Letters" into corresponding "Numbers"):

Hex to Binary Conversions								
A	8	4	2	1	8	4	2	1
B								
C	Left = 3				Right = C (12)			

- Begin the subtraction process on the "Left-Side" with the character "3":
  1. Ask the question "Is this a LETTER or a NUMBER?".
     - ➢ If character is a LETTER use conversion chart to change to correlated number and go to step #2.

Hex	Represents
A	10
B	11
C	12
D	13
E	14
F	15

     - ➢ If character is a NUMBER, continue to step #2.
  2. Can you subtract 8 from 3 = No (Which is "0" in binary).
     - ➢ Place a "0" in the "8-B" slot.
     - ➢ Continue to next "A-Row" number.
  3. Can you subtract 4 from 3 = No (Which is "0" in binary).
     - ➢ Place a "0" in the "4-B" slot.
     - ➢ Continue to next "A-Row" number.
  4. Can you subtract 2 from 3 = Yes (Which is "1" in binary).
     - ➢ Place a "1" in the "2-B" slot.
     - ➢ What remains of the original number?
       - o 3 − 2 = 1 (In decimal).
       - o Now use "1" as the number in the "C" slot.
     - ➢ Continue to next "A-Row" number.
  5. Can you subtract 1 from 1 = Yes (Which is "1" in binary).
     - ➢ Place a "1" in the "1-B" slot.
     - ➢ What remains of the original number?
       - o 0 (In decimal).

- All bits on the "Left Side" have been created resulting in "0011" which is the "nibble" for the hexadecimal character "3". Below:

		Hex to Binary Conversions						
A	8	4	2	1	8	4	2	1
B	0	0	1	1				
C	Left = 3				Right = C (12)			

- Now continue to do the same for the "Right Side" which has the character "C".
    1. Ask the question "Is this a LETTER or a NUMBER?".
        ➢ If character is a LETTER use conversion chart to change to correlated number and go to step #2.
            o The character "C" equals the decimal number "12". Insert "12" into the "C-Right" box and subtract all "B-Row" numbers from "12".

Hex	Represents
A	10
B	11
C	12
D	13
E	14
F	15

        ➢ If character is a NUMBER, continue to step #2.
    2. Can you subtract 8 from 12 = Yes (Which is "1" in binary).
        ➢ Place a "1" in the "8-B" slot.
        ➢ What remains of the original number?
            o 12 – 8 = 4 (In decimal).
            o Now use "4" as the number in the "C" slot.
        ➢ Continue to next "A-Row" number.
    3. Can you subtract 4 from 4 = Yes (Which is "1" in binary).
        ➢ Place a "1" in the "4-B" slot.

> What remains of the original number?
>   o 4 – 4 = 0 (In decimal).
>   o Now use "0" as the number in the "C" slot.
> ➤ Place a "0" in the "4-B" slot.
> ➤ Continue to next "A-Row" number.
  4. Can you subtract 2 from 0 = No (Which is "0" in binary).
> ➤ Place a "0" in the "2-B" slot.
> ➤ Continue to next "A-Row" number.
  5. Can you subtract 1 from 0 = No (Which is "0" in binary).

- All bits on the "Right Side" have been created resulting in "1100" which is the "nibble" for the hexadecimal character "C". The results appear as follows:

Hex to Binary Conversions								
A	8	4	2	1	8	4	2	1
B	0	0	1	1	1	1	0	0
C	Left = 3				Right = C (12)			

- This gives us the total answer that the hexadecimal combination "3C" = "00111100" in binary! Outstanding!!! Let's try another!

Take the following example: Given the MAC address of 23-3C-DD-AB-FE-72, what is the binary version of the 4th character set? Let's work the problem:
- 4th character set = "AB"
- Place the characters on the conversion chart as in the following (Remember to convert "Letters" into corresponding "Numbers"):

Hex to Binary Conversions								
A	8	4	2	1	8	4	2	1
B								
C	Left = A (10)				Right = B (11)			

- Begin the subtraction process on the "Left-Side" with the character "A":
  1. Ask the question "Is this a LETTER or a NUMBER?".
> ➤ We can see that the letter "A" has a decimal value of "10". Now continue to step #2.

Hex	Represents
A	10
B	11
C	12
D	13
E	14
F	15

2. Can you subtract 8 from 10 = Yes (Which is "1" in binary).
   - ➤ Place a "1" in the "8-B" slot.
   - ➤ What remains of the original number?
     - o 10 – 8 = 2 (In decimal).
     - o Now use "2" as the number in the "C" slot.
   - ➤ Continue to next "A-Row" number.
3. Can you subtract 4 from 2 = No (Which is "0" in binary).
   - ➤ Place a "0" in the "4-B" slot.
   - ➤ Continue to next "A-Row" number.
4. Can you subtract 2 from 2 = Yes (Which is "1" in binary).
   - ➤ Place a "1" in the "2-B" slot.
   - ➤ What remains of the original number?
     - o 2 – 2 = 0 (In decimal).
     - o Now use "0" as the number in the "C" slot.
   - ➤ Continue to next "A-Row" number.
5. Can you subtract 1 from 0 = No (Which is "1" in binary).
   - ➤ Place a "0" in the "1-B" slot.

- All bits on the "Left Side" have been created resulting in "1010" which is the "nibble" for the hexadecimal character "A" as in below:

	Hex to Binary Conversions							
A	8	4	2	1	8	4	2	1
B	1	0	1	0				
C	Left = A (10)				Right = B (11)			

- Now continue to do the same for the "Right Side" which has the character "B".
  1. Ask the question "Is this a LETTER or a NUMBER?".
     - If character is a LETTER use conversion chart to change to correlated number and go to step #2.
       - The character "B" equals the decimal number "11". Insert "11" into the "C-Right" box and subtract all "B-Row" numbers from "11".

Hex	Represents
A	10
B	11
C	12
D	13
E	14
F	15

  2. Can you subtract 8 from 11 = Yes (Which is "1" in binary).
     - Place a "1" in the "8-B" slot.
     - What remains of the original number?
       - 11 – 8 = 3 (In decimal).
       - Now use "3" as the number in the "C" slot.
     - Continue to next "A-Row" number.
  3. Can you subtract 4 from 3 = No (Which is "0" in binary).
     - Place a "0" in the "4-B" slot.
     - Continue to next "A-Row" number.
  4. Can you subtract 2 from 3 = Yes (Which is "1" in binary).
     - Place a "1" in the "2-B" slot.
     - What remains of the original number?
       - 3 – 2 = 1 (In decimal).
       - Now use "1" as the number in the "C" slot.
     - Continue to next "A-Row" number.
  5. Can you subtract 1 from 1 = Yes (Which is "1" in binary).
     - Place a "1" in the "1-B" slot.
     - What remains of the original number?
       - 1 – 1 = 0 (In decimal).

6. All bits on the "Right Side" have been created resulting in "1011" which is the "nibble" for the hexadecimal character "B". The results appear as follows:

Hex to Binary Conversions								
A	8	4	2	1	8	4	2	1
B	1	0	1	0	1	0	1	1
C	Left = A (10)				Right = B (11)			

- This give us the total answer that the hexadecimal combination "AB" = "10101011" in binary! Make up a few of your own and practice!

Because a MAC is unique and does not change, there is no major need to configure them (Unless creating more secure networks using IP version 6). In the field of server technology, however, there are requirements of understanding the construction of a MAC address. Although the hexadecimal characters are in groups of two,..there are actually two major sections of a MAC address. They are identified as the "First Six" and the "Last Six" characters as follows:

- **CC:CC:CC:MM:MM:MM**
- **CC-CC-CC-MM-MM-MM**

  - **First Six Characters (Represented by "CC")** = Represent the company or business which originally created the network interface such as "Dell", "IBM", etc. Each company which manufactures network interfaces are issued this unique number from Arpanet and the Department of Defense for security reasons. The MAC address of a device is often used to track down cyber criminals. All companies which create network interfaces keep records of all of them and where the card was installed or sold. You can insert the first six characters in an internet search and locate which company originally created or sold the network interface.

  - **Last Six Characters (Represented by "MM")** = identify the special make, model or creation date of the network interface. Often times, groups of the characters indicate that the model has special features such as "Wake on LAN" which would allow a computer to be turned on as long as it is connected to a network. Some high-end network interfaces are actually "mini-computers" which allow complete control of an entire computer even when the computer's power state is turned off.

Chapter 9
Network Utilities (Software, Commands and Tools)

Network Utilities (Software, Commands and Tools):

Working on networks often requires various tasks such as identification of devices, location of routes of travel and other elements common to communication networks. In our present day of technology, many operating systems and devices include applications and software-based tools to assist in network assessment and troubleshooting. Many of these tools require the familiarization with the use of the "CLI (Command Line Interface)". The following are commands which prove very useful when interacting or repairing network devices:

- **Hostname** = This command appears in Microsoft Operating Systems and Cisco Devices. Depending on the platform,..it can display the alpha-numeric identity of a system and/or change the identity of the system. The following are two of the utilizations of the command:
    - o Microsoft Server and Client platforms = Displays name of computer.
    - o Cisco Routers and Switches = Allows changing of a devices name.

- **Ipconfig** = Displays basic required network settings on Microsoft platforms. The command also has an optional modification of the command which will show a complete display of communication configurations. In order to use the enhanced features,.. additional words and characters must be appended to the command. The character which must be added is often called a "Forward Slash" or a "switch". The character visually is represented by using "/".
    - o Available switches:
        - ➤ All = Displays interfaces, protocols and settings.
        - ➤ Release = Informs the DHCP server the client no longer requires an IP address.
        - ➤ Renew = Requests an IP address from a DHCP server.

- **Ping** = Assesses the ability of one network device to contact another network device. Often used to assess if a computer can reach a printer or someplace on the internet. Much like other command line utilities, there are options available to manipulate the data reported by the "ping" command such as the following switches:
    - o –t = Continually attempt to find target IP until "cancel" command is executed (Ctrl+C).

o −n (Count) = Set number of times to attempt to contact target IP.
- **Pathping** = Displays the path and amount of message (Packet) loss occurring in transmission between a source system and destination system.
- **Tracert** = Displays the active path a node is using to contact another node. Will often display the following information about the nodes included in transit such as:
  o IP address
  o Fully Qualified Hostname
  o Time of transmission
- **Arp −a** = Displays IP addresses associated with MAC addresses of any hosts to which there was a communication.
- **Nbtstat −a** = Displays a computers hostname via its ip address.
- **Route print** = Used to display paths a node can use to pass traffic to various sections on a network. Primary syntax used on Microsoft Command Line applications.

Traditional Network Devices:

Networks today include many different devices supplying various functions such as shared files, live video, e-mail and many other functions. Regardless of the type, speed and expanse of the network,..there are a few devices which are traditionally part of all networks. The following are some devices typical on contemporary networks:
- **Simple Network (Hubs)** = Once the primary device which connected computers together into what is referred to as a "network". Due to their time of existence, hubs range from older 10BaseT to higher speed networks. There are even hubs which have BNC connectors to allow the connection to coaxial based networks. In addition to connecting network devices, they also have the purpose of extending the length of sections of a network to allow the coverage of a larger distance between computer systems. In the development of hubs, simple technologies were used to support the priority of connecting computers. Hubs separate PDU's by alternating when individual computers would have the opportunity to transmit via using CSMA/CD (Carrier Sense Multiple Access-Collision Detection). Using CSMA/CD, nodes on a network would all transmit as needed. If any PDU's enter the hub simultaneously (Called a "Collision), the hub generates a "jam signal" to all ports which terminates all communications and requires all computers connected to the hub to pause all transmissions for a random amount of time (In milliseconds). This

results in the following considerations when connecting network devices to a Hub:

- o **Single PDU processing** = A hub allows only a single PDU to pass thru it at any given time. Whichever device has the smaller time for its pause, would be allowed to transmit its data first, followed by the device with the next shortest pause interval.
- o **Divided bandwidth** = The maximum speed of a hub is related to the number of devices to which it is connected. Take the following for example.
  - ➤ 10 Port Hub rated at 10Mbps:
    - ❖ Connect 5 devices = Bandwidth is reduced to 2Mbps per connection.
    - ❖ Connect 10 devices = Bandwidth is reduced to 1Mbps per connection.
- o **Proximity Access** = Standard hubs have no network circuitry other then what supports passing PDU's. This limitation results in requiring that there is always easy access to a switch in order to address any problems it may experience. In addition, there are no options for remote management or security features.
  - ➤ The size of networks were extremely small compared to today's standards (In the 1990's, there might be only 25 computers in a 15-story dormitory holding 450 students). Today, that same dormitory might have a computer in every students' room. Hubs are now largely obsolete except for SOHO installations (Small Office-Home Office).
- **Simple Switch (SOHO-Switch)** = A SOHO (Small Office-Home Office) switch has all of the characteristics of a Hub but eliminates two disadvantages possessed by hubs:
  - o A switch will not divide bandwidth. If the switch is rated at 10Mbps, all ports will accept communications at that speed.
  - o Hubs allow multiple lines of communications between devices to occur simultaneously.
- **Corporate Switch** = Serving as the primary "distribution" node for a network, Switches are essential in the functioning of a major network. Corporate level Switches (Also called a Layer 2 Device) allow communication between thousands of systems simultaneously. Normally, switches exist on individual floors of building and continue to connect to one another in series. There is at least one switch which connects between

all the switches and the single router for the building which in turns connect to the ISP (Internet Service Provider). The following are some of the characteristic of Corporate level switches:

- o **Work out the box** = Switches will begin to route PDU's immediately. Plugging in most switches will allow electricity to flow and circuitry to pass packets between devices. In addition, some switches have PoE (Power over Ethernet). PoE indicates that the switch can transmit electricity over at least two of the wires in the category cable in order to supply power to devices connected to the cable such as wireless access points and Voice Over Internet Protocol telephone systems (VoIP).

- o **Remote Management** = A helpful feature of corporate switches is the ability to control the device via both a standard management protocol called "Telnet" and support control features using a internet browser-based "WebUI" (Web User Interface). This is a helpful feature because as long as the switch is powered on and has an IP address which can be contacted,..there is no need to be in the same physical location of the switch. Essentially, the network administrator can reach the device from anywhere in the world that has internet access.

- o **Configuration** = Although switches operate as soon as they have electricity, there are dozens of features available. Using a "corporate level" switch without customizing the device is essentially wasting thousands of dollars (Most corporate level switches cost above $3,000.00 each). The following are some of the aspects or functions available on corporate switches:

    - ➢ **Interface and Port types** = Normally there are about three types of interfaces available on switches. Any of which can be used to connect, configure or modify a switch. Many ports can have a username and password associated to prohibit unauthorized access or configuration of the switch. In addition, all of these passwords can be "Encrypted" (Process of making text and message illegible for unauthorized users). In addition to protecting the switch from users,..many Switch and Router operating systems allow placing credentials on the actual device so it can validate its identity to other Switches, Routers and network devices. Below are some of the ports normally on switches:

❖ **Console Port** = Primarily used to configure a switch but can also be used to upload files such as configurations and operating systems. Traditionally, this port has a "light blue" color to associate it with the console cable used to configure a router. There is another cable which mimics the design of a console cable called an "Aux" cable which can also be connected to this port.

❖ **Auxiliary Port (Aux)** = This port is a "legacy" connection used as a backup connection to the router in the event the device is failing. In addition, it can often be connected to a modem to temporally route traffic if the primary network connections were to fail. The port normally has a "black" color associating it with a console cable which is also "black".

❖ **Ethernet based ports** = These ports are used to connect network devices such as routers, computers, telephones, cameras, other switches, etc. The traffic that the switch processes travels along these ports. Depending on the age and cost of the switch,..they can vary in speed. Some of the speeds available at the time of writing this book are 10Mbps, 100Mbps, 1000Mbps (Often called "Gigabit Ethernet") and also 10-GigE (10,000 Mbps). The ports are often associated with the color "yellow".

❖ **Fiber Ports** = These ports support the connection of a fine material wire which allows the transmission of light from emitters on either end. Fiber cable is often used for extremely long distances between network devices such as building and cities. Fiber optic cable is also very fast with its slowest speed being 1000Mbps ("Gigabit Ethernet"). Fiber is also more stable because it is not susceptible to various types of interference such as EMI (Electric Magnetic Interference) or RFI (Radio Frequency Interference).

• **Routers** = Serving as the primary "Connection" node between building and separated networks. Routers (Also called a Layer 3 Device) allow communication between the different buildings and networks comprising the internet. Normally, each building has at least a single router which is connected to the "Core Switch" of a building one side and the Internet Service Provider (ISP) on the other. Essentially, routers have features similar to Switches such as telnet, ports, remote management, Backups, Command Line Interface (CLI), etc. plus additional features. The following are some of the characteristic of Routers:

- o **Must be Configured to operate** = Routers have absolutely no settings on them when they are brand new. They pass any traffic upon turning them on. Every route, pathway and access rule required on a router has to be manually initiated by a network technician. The command set used for routers is similar to those of a Switch with a few additional parameters.
- o **Routing Tables** = This is a list of how the router can move traffic thru and in between other networks.

Accessing a Shared Resource using UNC:

Universal Naming Convention (UNC) is a method for accessing shared resources on a network. Examples of resources could include items such as files, servers, internet sites, printers and many other network devices and locations. The resources are often printers, shared directories (folders) for group access, programs and many other resources. There are multiple access methods available when using a "UNC". Two of the most traditional is in using either the "Address Bar" of an Internet Browser (i.e., Internet Explorer, Firefox, Google Chrome, etc.) or what is often referred to as the "Search Field (Actually, a better name is the "Run Option") on the Start Menu on a computer using the Windows Operating System.

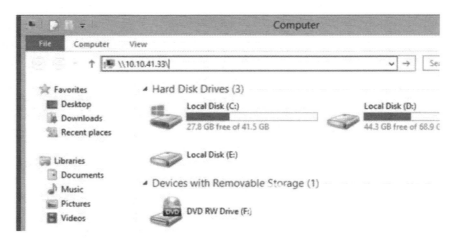

UNC has a specific order of how it must be written. The order consists of at least two or three sections which depends on the actual resource of which is being located. The two or three parts would be as follows:

- **Network Device Identity** = This would be either the hostname or IP address of the network device which holds the desired resource.
- **Directory Name** = The section within the device which contains a shared directory or device.
- **Resource name** = Actual name of the file, program or device such as a printer being accessed or initiated.

Each part of the UNC is separated by what is commonly referred to as a "backslash (\ ). The following is the syntax for a UNC:

- **\\DeviceName\DirectoryName\specific-file or Program**

The first two "backslashes (\\ )" command an operating system to "look inside of a network device. The third backslash tells an operating system to "go inside of a storage area". There can be multiple slashes which appear after this point which can mean either "go inside of the area inside of an area" and so on. The final part of the command will follow a backslash and ends with a filename and extension (i.e., ".bat", or ".exe", ".html", etc.) which tells an operating system to display a file or activate a program.

UNC's are normally used in LANs and Domains in order to provide access to frequently used file storage areas. In addition, UNC's often appear in automatic scripts and batch files to remove the necessity of users being required to memorize resource locations. An example of the use of a UNC in a batch file appears below. In this scenario, it is desired that a "Message of the day" file appears on a computer when anyone logs in. The message of the day was created in an application program called "Notepad" and saved in a "public folder" on the workstation so anyone may access the file. The file is called "dailylogin.bat" (The extension ".bat" identifies this file as a batch file). There are two methods which can be used to access the file in the storage area:
- **Option #1** = A user could use a "Search" or "Explorer" option and type the following UNC:
  - \\Unit01\hr\dailylogin.bat

- **Option #2** = A technician could place the file "dailylogin.bat" in the startup folder of the computer. When this occurs,..the batch file would activate without user intervention automatically every time a user logs into the computer.

The 2nd option is the method used more often in the field of computer technology. The following is another brief explanation of the UNC syntax:

- **"\\"** = Instructs an operating system to access a network device called "Unit04".
- **"\"** = Instructs an operating system to enter a director called "hr".
- **"\filename.ext"** = Instructs an operating system to activate a file with the name of "dailylong.bat."

What is a Virtual Private Network (VPN)?

Much commerce is carried out over the internet which is simply a number of multi-connected networks all over the world. In order for traffic to traverse the internet, thousands of network devices owned by individual organizations allow messages other than their own to pass thru their devices. Some of this data is very sensitive and must remain private, but at the same time, the only way to transmit this data is over public networks which creates a situation in which the information could possibly be viewed, altered or deleted. To control for these security issues, VPN processes are implemented. VPN's utilize a multitude of software and devices which allow secure data to travel thru public networks. Think of the message like a subway train which travels inside of a tunnel. The people are like the "data" sitting safely in a metal train car. Each user is unique and gets off of the train at a particular stop in the same condition in which they got on the train. Virtual Private Networks use various methods to protect data. The following are some brief examples of methods for protecting transmitted data:

- **Remote Access Services** = This is software which allows a person to literally view and control a computer system from a location physically removed from the actual computer. A person can be sitting in an office in Texas while controlling a computer in Pennsylvania. The person operating the computer is called a "Remote User". Every activity which can be performed while sitting directly in front of the computer can be done remotely. There are different categories of remote services as in the following:
  - ○ **Remote Assistance** = This is often used when a computer user is having difficulty with a program. What often occurs is that the user will contact "Help Desk" or "Tech Support" of some type. Often using an e-mail or a website, the user activates the connection. After the connection is made, the tech can see the screen of the computer user and give instructions on what the user must do to address the

need at present. If necessary, the user can grant the technician the right to control the mouse and keyboard as well as record the session.

- o **Remote Desktop** = This method is often used when a user is away from their office and requires access to files or programs on that office computer. This level of remote service allows the single user to use the computer as if they are at that location. They have full access to any programs on the computer as well as printers or any other devices locally connected to the computer. With this type of connection, the computer may or may not show that it is being operated remotely.

- o **Terminal Application Services** = This method is used by companies, businesses and organizations to streamline computer programs and possibly reduce the cost of applications. Essentially, a single (Or sometimes two servers for redundancy) will have all the programs which are used by a company. All the users in the company have computers but there are no programs on them (This type of computer is often called a "Thin Client"). When the user requires a program, they use their local computer to access the "Terminal Application Server" which offers them the use of the program without installing the software on the computer. Documents created in this manner can be stored either on the server or the local computer. An attractive feature of Terminal Application Services is that when applications or programs have to be updated or changed, the process occurs in one or two locations as opposed to servicing every computer on the network. A disadvantage to this method is often the cost of the server however because it has to be very high powered to support multiple almost simultaneous connections daily.

- **IPSec (Internet Protocol Security)** = This is a method of assuring the source and destination of data. Remember, all data which traverses a network is broken into different types of PDU's (Protocol Data Units). Within a unit, there is normally some indicator of the source of a PDU such as the original devices IP address. Essentially, communication network devices can be configured to only accept messages from a particular group of sending and receiving IP addresses. Any other PDU's are ignored.

- **Authentication** = With this method, the actual PDU will include a password or username combination to initiate communications between devices. Both the sender and receiver are configured with usernames and passwords which allow a "handshake" proving the identity of one another. After the handshake occurs, the two devices allow the flow of data.

- **Encryption** = This is the process of protecting data from being viewed by those other than who the data is intended. Encryption often utilizes two different methods such as the following:
  - **Symmetric** = Both users have the same key for scrambling and unscrambling a message.
  - **Asymmetric** = Uses pairs of keys (At least two keys called **"Private"** and **"Public").** To encrypt a message, each user has their own private key. Then the message can be sent to other users in a more private format. Any user who must decrypt a message must have the original users public key which is distributed to specific users in various methods (Key Server, E-mail, Encryption Key Services, etc.).

- There are multiple types of encryptions but most are related to the base unit of data on computer networks defined as a "bit ("0" or a "1"). All computer data and communications are a collection of bits known as "binary numbers" (Such as the collection "00000011" which is the binary code for the decimal number "3" or "10000010" which is the binary code for the decimal number "130"). When encryption is involved, the arrangement of bits will be "scrambled" or "altered" in some way. In addition, some encryption software inserts "nonsense characters" which cannot be converted to anything. Encryption software might change the arrangement of bits to produce a different number. When this occurs,..essentially there is a "locking" process which changes the bits, and a "Key' process which returns the collection of bits to their original format. Let's simulate an "Eight-Bit Encryption" process for the number "130" as an example:
  - **Step #1 (Locking process called "Encryption")** = Change every 8 bits of a message into the reverse of the bit which exists in the message. The message changes from "10000010" to "01111101" which is a totally different number (If you are curious, it is "125").
  - **Step #2 (Transmission process)** = Message is sent to recipient via available transport method (i.e., FTP, E-Mail, Text, etc.).
  - **Step#3 (Receiver uses Key (Called "Decryption)** = Decryption key Change every 8 bits of a received message into the reverse of the bit which now appears. The message changes from "01111101" back to the original "10000010".

- In order for encryption to operate, it is necessary for the "Lock and Key" process to be accessible for both the sender and receiver of messages. When this arrangement exists,..it is often called a **"PKI (Public Key Infrastructure).** PKI is a security feature often used when password and username protection may not be adequate. Using either a PKI service or on-site servers it is possible to create, store, and disable key-and-lock agreements (Also called "Security Certificates"). Using these servers, it is possible to send key-and lock combinations to specific users so they can use the keys to protect any data which is stored or transmitted over the internet. Using a PKI requires two elements. A public key and a private key (Which actually functions as the "Lock"). The following are brief examples of the two elements:

- **Private Key** = This key is owned by a specific user. The code of this key will encrypt any data sent by this particular user. All users will have a totally unique Private key which must be combined with the Public Key when encrypt a particular user's messages or files.

- **Public Key** = This part of the process is made available to everyone involved in the transmission of the secure data. This is the key which is used to decrypt the data. It is usually based on a mathematical formula and scrambles the bits in groups of 16, 32, 64, 128 or greater. The higher the number of bits, the more secure the message. The disadvantage to the higher the number of bits,...the more processing time required to decrypt a message.

Chapter 10
Hackers vs. Crackers

Hackers vs. Crackers

There are many conversations in the cyber-security and network world in reference to the term "Hackers" and also the lesser-known term of "Crackers". Although there is no need to go into intense detail on the similarities and differences in the terms, it is appropriate to them give them mention in a book which examines network technology. Both terms are attempting to define experts in the computer field who have a great understanding of computer language (Often called "computer code") and network communication software (Often called "protocols"). Utilizing this knowledge, these computer experts can participate in two distinct activities:

- **"Hacker"** = Identify and exploit areas in which a computer or network system can be damaged or compromised. These persons often work for businesses which create options for network security or antivirus software. Their goal is to assure the continued operation of a business and to safeguard all data maintained and services provided by the business or company. Computer experts in this area are also often called "White Hats".

- **"Cracker"** = Participate in compromising or damaging computer network devices and systems. The term originated from the term "Safe Cracker" (Person who would rob vaults in banks, stores and other businesses). Primarily working as "contractors" or "individual/group" entities, they have the goal of participating in malicious activities concerning computer data, services or operation. In contrast with hackers, they are often referred to as "Black Hats". Examples of malicious activities would include the following:

  - **Stopping or destroying computer data using virus or network attacks (Trojans, phishing, DoS, etc.).**
  - **Accessing and distributing confidential data (Movies, credit card and personal data, etc.)**
  - **Stopping an internet business from being accessed by users (i.e., Netflix, Sony PlayStation, etc.).**

Although, there is a distinction made between "Hackers" and "Crackers", their abilities are the same but their motives define their classification. Depending on the situation and affiliations, they could be the "good guys" or the "bad guys" depending on the perspective and the matter at hand. There are many movies which attempt to display the story of the "person who hacks into a computer system and later gains a really good job in the computer field." Although this is a possibility, remember always that accessing computer data without appropriate authorization and approval may be viewed as a crime punishable by termination or prison time. In the event you are involved accessing computer data for yourself or a company, make sure you are represented by a lawyer. Protect yourself at all times.

What is a "Computer Virus" or "Malware"?

A virus is a program which was created to carry out malicious activities on a computer. Literally a programmer used computer code to create a set of instructions which will negatively affect a computer or the user on a computer. The negative effect could be stealing data, stopping the use of a computer or file and even destroying the operating systems or the hardware on a computer. Viruses come in multiple forms but they all have at least two elements in common which are damaging effect and ability to replicate (Duplicate itself in different places).

Similar to a disease that can be spread from person-to-person by contact, a computer virus spreads between computer systems using some type of transmission or common contact area such as a file, storage area (Flashdrive, SD card, Website, etc.) or even an e-mail. All viruses do not immediately attack a computer or user. Often time,..many viruses' stay inactive on a system until the user performs a specific activity or a "timer" of some type activates the virus. The only way to protect your computer from virus attacks is to think about it like your home and use the same protections:

- **Turn away unknown strangers at your door** = If an e-mail comes to you that you do not recognize, delete it. Do not open it.
- **Keep doors locked when away and turn on security system** = Install Firewall and Antivirus software to stop virus from coming in via websites and documents as well as removing those which made it past the firewalls.
- **Always know your neighbors** = Be aware of the actual identities of people who send or exchange data with your computer. Keep your antivirus system up to date.

There are many antivirus utilities on the market. There is no "best one" but keep in mind,.. "The more locks you have on your door,..the more difficult it will be for the thief". My analogy here is that the more you spend on an antivirus,..the greater protection it offers. There is a balance, however. The higher the level of antivirus and firewall you have on your computer, the more resources it will use (Such as the CPU and RAM). If you place an expensive antivirus program on a cheap computer,..the computer will operate extremely slow. Match your antivirus with the abilities on your computer (Commonly referred to as the

"Requirements" or "Specifications") to assure that the antivirus you install will not affect your computer worse than actually having a virus. The following are some Types and categories of Viruses:

- **Spyware** = This term is used to describe software which is installed without a computer owner's permission in order to gather private information and make it available to the owner of the spyware (Often by reporting the data in the form of an e-mail). The information could include, internet activities, visited websites, keystrokes (also called "keylogging"), saved documents and passwords. Similar to Spyware is a variant called "Adware" which will cause a computer browser homepage to change or initiate visiting unknown websites without the users request or display commercials randomly on a computer. The most well-known cause of Adware is when a user attempts to download a "free" software not knowing that the condition is the installation of software which will force your browser to use a search engine not selected by you.

- **Trojan** = This virus is created to look innocent. Often it will look like a normal document such as a "docx" or "pdf. It is also often disguised as an e-mail attachment. Traditionally, Trojans do not replicate automatically and require a user to perform some type of activity to activate them. Once activated by a user,..a Trojan virus can perform a number of different attacks on a computer system such as recording the keys pressed on a keyboard, deleting files, changing filenames or making files invisible (Or what we call "Hidden").

- **Worm** = Worms travel between network devices in order to send copies of data back to the creator of the Worm. Normally this data is credit cards, social security numbers, customer databases, etc. The data is often deposited on a website or contained in a hidden e-mail. Worms often hide their existence and create "backdoors (Method of accessing an operating system or device without the owners' knowledge) which a malicious program can utilize to continue to compromise data records and systems. An important aspect involving a Worm is that is normally "self-replicating" which means that it copies itself and travels between computers systems without the intervention of a programmer. Once launched on a network, until erased, a Worm is totally self-sufficient.

- **Macro** = The name for this virus originates from the function available in programs to automatically perform a number of tasks after activating a key combination or clicking on a single icon. When the macro is a virus, however,..the tasks could include inserting lines of text in the header or footer of every document printed. A macro virus installs itself into other programs and will replicate itself into any files or documents created with that particular program. Another example would be when an e-mail is sent to a user,..commercials or advertisement from the creator of the Macro virus would also be sent to the recipient.

- **Hijackware (Also called "Redirection Malware")** = This type of virus modifies the settings of internet browsers such as Internet Explorer, Google Chrome and Firefox. The results of getting Hijackware are evident when a user's internet search is randomly redirected to Web sites other than those for which were being searched. Often time, the home page of the user or the default search engine is also changed. Unknown bookmarks, pornographic pop-ups and random commercials are often symptoms of Hijackware. There have been a number of versions of Hijackware which totally locks a computer and attempts to force the user to send money to the creator of the virus in order to be given an unlock code. Most often,…the unlock code is never sent and the data as well as the money paid is forever lost.

Active System Attacks Explanations

In addition to the dangers of viruses, there are persons who use their knowledge of computer code and software to create applications to actively attack and disable computers and entire networks. These individuals can literally access a computer system and attempt to compromise network settings. A more popular method is to create software which will automatically attack networks without user intervention. The following are some of the types and categories of Active System Attacks:

- **DoS** (Denial-of-Service) = This occurs when an attacker makes a computer or other network services unable to be used. Examples of a DoS attack would be if a user's e-mail inbox constantly receives new items and fills to its limit. This would stop additional e-mails from being accepted. If the DoS is based on an internet service an example would be if hundreds of computers constantly and repeatedly made requests to Google or Yahoo which had no answer. The search services for those companies would be overwhelmed attempting to create responses for questions which had no answers, resulting in not addressing new legitimate searches made by actually users. When multiple computers are being used in the attack,..another name is used for the denial. It is called a DDoS (Distributed Denial of Service).

- **Spoofing** = Spoofing is the activity of a network intrusion or attack when a computer or system impersonates the appearance of an approve system on a network. Many computer networks have methods of authentication (Proof of identity) which is used to allow computers access to a network or specific resources on a network. Once the attacker successfully impersonates an approved system,..multitudes of attacks can occur such as DoS, confidential data collection and permanent network destruction. Oftentimes, this authentication is based upon impersonating one or more of the elements required for network access:
  - **IP Address**
  - **MAC Address**
  - **Hostname**
  - **Telephone Number**
  - **E-mail Address**
  - **Global Position (GPS)**

- **Brute Force** = This type of attack occurs when a number of randomly selected numbers, usernames, passwords and phrases are attempted to access a computer or network resource. The process is totally "Trial and Error". Either an actual person can physically attempt a brute force attack or software can be used to attempt thousands of random combinations.

- **Dictionary Attack** = This type of attack requires the use of some type of database of specific numbers, usernames, passwords and phrases. The elements have some form of association as well as a specific order of which combinations will be use first and last. The reason it is called a dictionary attack is due to the predetermined numbers, usernames, passwords and phrases selection much like that which appears in a dictionary.

- **Social Engineering** = Social engineering is the art of manipulating people and uses human interaction in order to derive confidential information. Using everyday seemingly normal conversations, the attacker is attempting to gain information such as passwords, confidential data locations or information on the physical location of servers or even information about what security measure are used in a company, business or organization.

Social engineering involves face-to-face, telephone or other verbal communications

- **Baiting** = Making convenient access to a device such as a flash drive to a computer user who the "Bad Guy" wants to compromise. The person who picks up the flashdrive and uses it does not know that the flashdrive has software on it which will compromise the computer in various ways such as automatically installing monitoring or remote access software.

- **Phishing** = This occurs via telephone, e-mail and text messaging. Essentially, a message is received informing of some important occurrence (Lottery Winner, Bank Account Confirmation, System Update). Somewhere in the communication, there will be a request to send the message sender some type of confidential data (i.e., Username, Password, Account Number, etc.). Once the data is sent, the attacker now has the ability to either steal data or launch attacks against the user's servers.

- **Steganography** = This is not an actual "attack" as much as it is a method for confidential data to be transmitted from a network in secret. The process of hiding messages in videos or pictures. In computer technology, messages can be hidden within a digital photo or video. Both the sender and receiver must possess similar software to either insert messages or reveal messages. There are many different steganography programs available which range from no charge to very expensive.

Security Methods for Servers, Networks and User Accounts

Although there is no perfect method of protecting data, computers, server and networks,..there are a number of "best practices". These are methods advocated by computer professionals in areas of cyber-security based upon experiments, trials and even studies of cyber-attacks. This list is not all-inclusive but serve as a starting point for security discussions.

- **Strong Passwords** = A method often utilized in basic level security of a user account or computer is via using an account which combines a "username (Collection of letters which represent a person, i.e., a person named "Bill White" might have a username of "BWhite")" and a password (A combination of keyboard characters known only by a particular user). It was thought at one time that the more characters you have in a password, the more secure it is. After much studies, it was found out that by combining the various characters available on a keyboard actually increases levels of security. Following that philosophy, Microsoft released recommendations for using what is called a "strong password". This type of password includes the following elements.

- o **8 or more characters**
- o **Random letters and numbers (Not in typical order such as "ABC", "123" or "QWE".**
- o **Both Uppercase and Lowercase Letters**
- o **Utilizing symbols when possible (Such as #, *, &, @, etc.).**

- **Firewall (Really per computer)** = A firewall actually a very generic term. Traditionally, it describes a software or device which monitors access to a computer (Sometimes, it may be part of a DMZ for an entire network). Essentially, the firewall will look for activity which falls outside of a "baseline" (Standard for normal computer activity). When an activity outside of the baseline occurs, the firewall can automatically disconnect the connection or inform a computer user of the activity. As a comparison, think of a computer as a very popular "nightclub" with a dress code requiring a tie for males. At the door of the club, there are staff members who assure all males have ties. If a male attempts to enter without a tie, this would be "outside of the baseline" which will either cause the club staff to reject the male or ask management if the eager club goer should be allowed to enter.

- **Network or Server "Baseline"** = A "Baseline" is a term used to describe the condition of a network based on a history of normal operations. The condition would include amount of e-mail traffic, number of users accessing a network at a particular time, amount of bandwidth being utilized, even number and type of help-desk calls received daily. The baseline is important because it can be used to differentiate between normal activity and abnormal. Software monitoring a network will notice and indicate changes to normal traffic far quicker than users. In fact, if a networks connection to the internet begins to deteriorate, it will be noticed long before the connection totally fails. It is better to catch the failure before the work of users is affected. In this way, the network administrator can attempt to isolate the problem concerning if it is an equipment failure, change because of an upgrade or an actual attack by a malicious user or malware. There are some primary categories of software used to identify baselines as well as isolating problem factors such cyber-related attacks. The following are those categories:

- **IDS (An Intrusion Detection System)** = This is a device or software which actively compares present activities to a baseline concerning accessing other network devices and resources such as servers, file storage areas, etc. Many times, it will not be a single element, but might include a combination of firewall, antivirus and DMZ monitoring configurations. In addition, traditionally the IDS will have a feature which will notify the person(s) in charge of network security, often using a text message, flashing lights on a control interface and sometimes an audible alert (Bell or Horn). Higher versions will often create a log or display of access violations including user, date and even the computers' location.

- **IPS (Intrusion Prevention System)** = This is often a combination of firewall, antivirus and DMZ settings based upon known system attack types. These attacks could be protocol based (RDP on networks which do not require it) or signature-based (When line of code attempts to execute on a network device). The primary consideration of IPS is understanding that it only protects against attack types which have been configured in its performance code. Any new variation of the attack or code might be able to slip thru an IPS. For this reason, it is best practice to have the IDS strongly associated with the IPS.

DMZ (Often called a "Demilitarized Zone") = Many companies provide services on the internet in our present day. Some companies such as "Facebook", "Netflix" and many other organizations have computer networks all over the world. Many international companies and banks also participate in various types of trade and commerce on the internet. The only way to access these networks and servers is to have some type of permanent connection with the internet. That "door" to the internet swings both ways, however. Anytime a company allows access to their network for paying customers and remote employees, there is the opportunity for unwelcomed visitors who may attempt to access servers and files located within a network. Due to the potential for network attacks,..companies and businesses often create a "protection area" which exists between the company's primary network and the outside world. In network terms, this protection area is called a "DMZ (Demilitarized zone)". DMZ's primarily protect entire networks. In computer security, a DMZ or demilitarized zone (sometimes referred to as a perimeter network) is a physical or logical subnetwork that contains and exposes an organization's external-facing services to an untrusted network, usually a larger network such as the Internet. The purpose of a DMZ is to add an additional layer of security to an organization's local area network (LAN);

an external network node can access only what is exposed in the DMZ, while the rest of the organization's network is firewalled.

A DMZ would have a collection of various servers and devices which protect a network from damage or attack from both inside and outside the network. There might be servers which stop unrequested e-mails (Often called "Spam") from entering the inbox of users. Sometimes there are special filters on servers which will stop company users from visiting pornographic websites. There are also servers which would stop hidden messages from being sent to other servers from within the network.

Chapter 11
Example Labs and
Configurations

Example Labs and Configurations:

The following are some practical labs illustrating some methods of configuring network devices. All listed labs and exercises were created by using actual functioning PC's, Routers and Switches. Purchasing actual Routers and Switches is possible at a fraction of the cost by using "EBay" and "Amazon". Simulation software is also another option for practicing network technology tasks and activities. At the time of this book, there were a number of vendors who supplied simulation software such as "Boson NetSim", "NetSimK" and "Packet Tracer". If simulation software is used,... some commands used on real devices may not work. Be sure to evaluate simulation software's available functions prior to attempting each lab.

Each lab builds on the prior labs so it is essential that they are completed in the order in which they appear. In addition, each lab increases in challenge levels and repeats prior activities in order to teach procedures and commands thru repetition. As the writer of this text,..I would highly recommend completing each lab three times prior to starting the subsequent lab. When performing the lab for the third time, attempt to do so without any notes or instructions.

PC-Hub-PC:

This is one of the first types of networks created for home offices. We will use two workstations and a hub. Afterwards we will confirm communications between the PC's. You will need the following for the lab:
1) Two PC's with hardware ethernet connections (Not wireless!)
2) PC's with Windows 7/8 or 10.
3) 4 10/100/100 port hub (Inexpensive unit from 3Com or NetGear).
4) Two straight ethernet cables.
   o Hardware Setup:
     □ Connect one straight cable from a PC to the hub.
     □ Connect the remaining straight cable from the hub to the other PC.
   o Boot up each computer and access the command line interface (CLI).
     □ Go to the "Start" menu".
     □ Click one time into the "Search" field.
     □ Type "cmd" or "command" and the CLI "black-box" will appear.

- o Determine the network settings of each PC by doing the following:
  - ☐ Type "ipconfig" in the command line option:
  - ☐ At least three lines of text will appear displaying the following:
    - IPv4 address = This may appear as either of the following:
      - ➢ "0.0.0.0 = Means that the computer has not derived an IP address as of yet.
      - ➢ 169.254.x.y = This is APIPA. The "x" and the "y" can be any number between 0 and 255. The will be different on each PC.
    - IPv6 "link-local" address = Fe80: (Many numbers. This is for later so don't give this much attention).
    - Subnet Mask = This attempts to identify the groups of computers which are associated for communications.
      - ➢ It should be 255.255.255.0
    - Default Gateway = This should be blank at present.
  - o This first command attempts to show only "active" settings. To see all settings and connections regardless of status,.the "ipconfig" command must be modified with a switch such as "/all". It is performed in the following manner, "ipconfig[space]/all". This command results in additional hardware and software settings. Settings important for our lab would include the following:
    - ☐ **DNS Server** = The device on the network which matches ip addresses to the hostname of systems.
    - ☐ DHCP Server = The device which distributes IP addresses to devices on a network (Will be empty for this lab).
    - ☐ **Hostname** = Written name of computer.
    - ☐ **Physical Address** = The hexadecimal mac address for the network adaptors on the system.
  - o **Establish connections between PC's** = Using a command line tool, we can ascertain if the PC's can communicate with each other. Prior to attempting this command, assure all firewall's are off. If you are using a Windows PC. You can use a single

command which will turn all firewalls off. To do so, activate the CLI and perform the command "netsh advfirewall set allprofiles state off". The command will respond with "OK" when the firewalls has been disabled. To re-enable the firewalls, simply type the same command but replace "off" with "on". (Note, this command will only work if Windows is controlling the firewall and not a third-party software such as Symantec or McAfee). After the firewall is down, we can attempt communication tests. Perform the following steps:

- ☐ Identify each computer as computer "A" and computer "B".
- ☐ Using "ipconfig" record the ip address of each computer. Use the following as an example (Note if IP address reads "0.0.0.0" go to "Static Address Configuration):
  - Computer "A" = 169.254.182.10
  - Computer "B" = 169.254.112.20
- ☐ Access the CLI of computer "A".
- ☐ Type "ping" and the IP address of computer "B" such as "ping 169.254.112.20".
- ☐ The results should be between 3 and 5 sentences reading as follows:
  - Reply from 169.254.112.20: bytes = 32 time=TTL= 32.
    - ➢ Just know that this means "Hey, I found the other computer!"
  - If you get any sentences stating "Reply timeout" that means the target system cannot be located.
- o **Static Address Configuration** = using APIPA is somewhat problematic for many of our labs, so we should use a static address. Depending on the operating system on the computer, there are different ways to access the network interface. We will use a simple command line to configure our network adaptor.
  - ☐ **Identify network interface** = Type in "ipconfig" and the active interface will appear with name of the interface and the ip address it is presently using.

```
C:\Users\rspencer>ipconfig
Windows IP Configuration

Wireless LAN adapter Wireless Network Connection 3:

   Media State . . . . . . . . . . . : Media disconnected
   Connection-specific DNS Suffix  . :

Wireless LAN adapter Wireless Network Connection 2:

   Connection-specific DNS Suffix  . :
   Link-local IPv6 Address . . . . . : fe80::b9d6:9590:92fb:3c8%15
   IPv4 Address. . . . . . . . . . . : 192.168.1.173
   Subnet Mask . . . . . . . . . . . : 255.255.255.0
   Default Gateway . . . . . . . . . : 192.168.1.10
```

- ☐ Using the interface name, we can configure an IP address on the interface using the following context:

```
Administrator: C:\Windows\system32\cmd.exe

C:\>netsh interface ipv4 set address name="local area connection 2" static 172.1
6.20.10 255.255.255.0 172.16.20.1
```

- • netsh interface ipv4 set address name="NameOfYourAdaptor" static ip-address subnet-mask gateway". For our lab, go to computer "A" and perform the following:
  - ➤ netsh interface ipv4 set address name="NameOfYourAdaptor" static 172.16.20.10 255.255.255.0 172.16.20.1
  - ➤ Type "Ipconfig", again and check to see if the settings are what you expected.
- ☐ Go to computer "B" and perform the following:
  - ➤ netsh interface ipv4 set address name="NameOfYourAdaptor" static 172.16.20.20 255.255.255.0 172.16.20.1 (We have changed the last octet of the IP address to make "B" unique from "A".
  - ➤ Type "Ipconfig", again and check to see if the settings are what you expected.
- ☐ Execute pings between computer "A" and "B" looking for positive replies.
  - ➤ If you get positive replies,..success!! You have created your first local area network! If not successful, check your firewalls and the IP addresses you placed on the individual computers.

☐ To return an interface to dhcp, perform the following:
  ➤ netsh interface ipv4 set address
    name="NameOfYourAdaptor" source=dhcp

Terminal Emulator to Switch

This lab will require the knowledge from all aspects of the previous lab. If you did not complete it,..go back because instructions in this lab require the knowledge from the previous labs. Items required for this lab will be as follows:

1) Console cable
2) Straight cable
3) PC
4) Corporate level switch (2600 or above with CLI).
5) Terminal Emulation Software (Teraterm/HyperTerminal/Putty) installed:

o Before starting, give the PC the following network settings:
  ☐ IP Address = 172.16.20.10
  ☐ Subnet Mask = 255.255.255.0
  ☐ Default Gateway = 172.16.20.1

o Switch Connection Process:

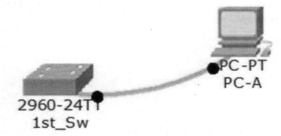

o Connect the end of the console cable to the PC using the "Serial" interface:

o Connect the "RJ45" end into the Switch Console Port (Highlighted in "light" blue).

o Turn on terminal emulator and select correct port.

o Hit the "Enter" key and you should be in " --- System Configuration Dialog ---"

```
--- System Configuration Dialog ---

Continue with configuration dialog? [yes/no]: no
```

o Type "N" or "No" to all questions (About two or three). After
  you type the last "No" the system will check interfaces and
  circuitry and seem to stop. It is only waiting for your input.
o Hit the "Enter" key and you should be in "User" mode
  (Indicated by the ">" prompt).
o Type "Enable" or "en" and hit "enter" key to place you into
  "Privileged" mode (Indicated by the "#" prompt).
o Evaluate the device by typing the following commands:
  □ Sh ver = Displays the following:
    ➢ RAM usage
    ➢ Operating System Version
    ➢ Interfaces
    ➢ Platform
    ➢ Processor
    ➢ And present configuration register setting (We will
      talk about this item later in the book).

```
Cisco WS-C2950-24 (RC32300) processor (revision C0) with 21039K byte

Processor board ID FHK0610Z0WC
Last reset from system-reset
Running Standard Image
24 FastEthernet/IEEE 802.3 interface(s)

63488K bytes of flash-simulated non-volatile configuration memory.
Base ethernet MAC Address: 0030.F218.E82A
Motherboard assembly number: 73-5781-09
Power supply part number: 34-0965-01
Motherboard serial number: FOC061004SZ
Power supply serial number: DAB0609127D
Model revision number: C0
Motherboard revision number: A0
Model number: WS-C2950-24
System serial number: FHK0610Z0WC
Configuration register is 0xF
```

  □ **Show run** = Will display, descriptions, customizations,
    interfaces and all configurations presently running on
    them.

- **Sh ip int brief** = Will display a small listing of network interfaces and their status.
- Begin the process for customizing the Switch with the following options:
  - Avoiding unknown command errors:
    1) Switch>Enable
    2) Switch (Config t) (Moves into go Global Configuration).
    3) Switch (Config#) no ip domain-lookup
    4) Switch (Config#) end <enter> (This will move curser back to "User" mode.
  - Naming the Switch:
    1) Switch>Enable
    2) Switch (Config t) (Moves into go Global Configuration).
    3) Switch (Config#) Hostname First_Floor_Switch (Immediately changes name of switch).
    4) Switch (Config#) end <enter> (This will move curser back to "User" mode.
  - Giving the switch an IP address:
    1) Switch> En
    2) Switch#
    3) Switch# Config t
    4) Switch (Config#) int vlan 1
    5) Switch (Config-if#) ip add 172.16.10.1 255.255.255.0
    6) Switch (Config-if#) no shut (This is an optional command)
    7) Switch (Config-if#) end <enter>
    8) Perform a "show run" or "Sh ip int brief" to see the IP listed.
  - Test connection between Switch and PC. From the CLI on the switch execute a "ping" to the PC:
    1) First_Floor_S1> ping 172.16.20.2
    2) You should get a total of 5 exclamation points which = 100% successful. Other indications you could receive:
       - "!" = 20% Successful
       - "." = 20% Unsuccessful

> "U.U.U.U." = Destination unreachable or misconfiguration.

3) Often the first time, only 60% is successful because device is learning network. Ping again and 100% should be the second result.

☐ **Removing an IP address:**
1) Switch#Config-t (Moves into go Global Configuration).
2) Switch (Config)# int vlan 1
3) Switch (Config-if#) no ip add
4) Switch (Config-if#) no shut (This is an optional command)
5) Switch (Config-if#) end <enter>

Switch-to-Switch:

This lab allows communication between two switches. To complete the tasks, you must be familiar with all previous labs. Remember to use commands to check your work (i.e., "Sh Run" and "Show IP int brief", etc.).

o Connect a Cross-over cable between the switches (Best practice although newer switches will auto-configure if a straight-cable is used).

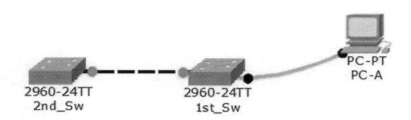

2960-24TT
2nd_Sw

2960-24TT
1st_Sw

PC-PT
PC-A

o Configure first switch as follows:
☐ Hostname = 1ST_Sw
☐ IP Settings = 172.16.10.3 Netmask 255.255.255.0
o Configure second switch as follows:
☐ Hostname = 2ND_Sw
☐ IP Settings = 172.16.10.4 Netmask 255.255.255.0
o Ping between the two switch IP addresses.
o If pings fail, assure that devices are connected using Cisco Discovery Protocol.
☐ On "1st_Sw enter "Privileged mode (#)".
☐ Type "sh cdp neigh"

□　A display should appear stating that your neighbor is "2nd_Fl" and the port to which it is connected.
　o　If you want to see a more detailed description, type in the expanded version of the CDP command,"Sh cdp neigh detail".
　　　□　The result will display addition information such as IP address, operating system, platform, etc.

Switch and Router Passwords:

If a switch or router can be physically touched it is susceptible to access and reconfiguration. There are some methods which would make unauthorized access more difficult. We can configure some of these methods in the following ways:

　o　**Console Password** = This password protects the physical port used to connect the console cable (Also called "Rolled Cable" with the color of "Light Blue"). Before any terminal emulation software will allow access to a network device,..a password must be entered and accepted. The following is the configuration process:
　　　□　1ST_Sw# sh run (Look for the statement which starts "…line con 0")

```
line con 0
!
line vty 0 4
  login
line vty 5 15
  login
```

　　　□　1ST_Sw# Config t
　　　□　1ST_Sw (Config)# line con 0
　　　□　1ST_Sw (Config)# Login (A message appears that a password is required but not set)
　　　□　1ST_Sw (config-line)# Password getcon
　　　□　1ST_Sw (config-line)# End
　　　□　1ST_Sw#Sh run (Look for password related statements under "line con 0")
　　　□　Now turn off TeraTerm and re-plugging the console cable.
　　　□　Restart Teraterm and hit enter (Notice a "User Access Verification" prompt appears).
　　　　❖　Note: it will not show letters as you type.

- ☐ Type in "getcon" and you are now in user mode of the switch.

- o **Enable Password** = This will stop users if they try to move from "user>" to "privileged#" mode. The following is the process:
  - ☐ 1ST_Sw# sh run (Toward the "top half" of the screen, you will see no password statements).

```
Current configuration : 971 bytes
!
version 12.1
no service timestamps log datetime msec
no service timestamps debug datetime msec
no service password-encryption
!
hostname switch
```

  - ☐ 1ST_Sw# Config t
  - ☐ 1ST_Sw (Config)# enable password geten
  - ☐ 1ST_Sw (config-line)# End
  - ☐ 1ST_Sw# Sh run (Look for password towards top of readout)

```
Current configuration : 995 bytes
!
version 12.1
no service timestamps log datetime msec
no service timestamps debug datetime msec
no service password-encryption
!
hostname switch
!
enable password geten        ⬅
```

  - ☐ 1ST_Sw# exit
  - ☐ Hit enter
  - ☐ 1ST_Sw> enable (Notice a "Password" prompt appears).
  - ☐ Note, it will not show letters as you type.
  - ☐ Type in "getin" and press enter to access user mode of the switch.

- o **Telnet Password** = This allows remote access to a switch or router using an IP address. Prior to configuring telnet, an

"Enable" password must be set. The process for telnet passwords are as follow:

- ☐ 1ST_Sw# sh run (Look for the statement which starts "…line vty 0 4 (Or 0 15)")

  ```
  line con 0
  !
  line vty 0 4
   login
  line vty 5 15
   login
  ```

- ☐ 1ST_Sw# Config t
- ☐ 1ST_Sw (Config)# line vty 0 4
- ☐ 1ST_Sw (Config)# Login (Messages may appears stating a password is required but not set on any lines)
- ☐ 1ST_Sw (config-line)# Password gettel
  - ❖ Note: Notice the prompted changed to "(config-line)#".
- ☐ 1ST_Sw (config-line)# End
- ☐ 1ST_Sw# Sh run (Look for password related statements under "line vty 0 4")
- ☐ You must test the connection from another device such as a switch or a router. The other device must be able to successfully "ping" the switch or router you are attempting to access.
- ☐ 2ND_Sw # Ping 172.16.10.3 and wait for "!!!!! (100% Successful communications - Assuming this is the IP address of the switch we have enabled with telnet)."
- ☐ 2ND_Sw# telnet 172.16.10.3 (Notice a "User Access Verification" prompt appears).
- ☐ Type in "gettel" and press enter.
- ☐ Note, it will not show letters as you type.
- ☐ Notice the prompt turns to the name of the switch we were attempting to access.
- ☐ 1ST_Sw>en
- ☐ You are now accessing the configurations of the other switch.

- o **Enable Secret** = All of the prior passwords are able to be read. The term for this is "cleartext". This is a security concern since configurations are often printed out to check settings. In order make systems more secure, we can restrict access to "privileged" mode by modifying the appearance of the enable password to make it illegible. The term is called "encryption". In order to do this, you utilize the following method:
  - ☐ 1ST_Sw# Config t
  - ☐ 1ST_Sw (Config)# enable secret kitty
  - ☐ 1ST_Sw (Config)# end
  - ☐ 1ST_Sw# sh run (The password entry will now look like a random string of letters and numbers).

```
!
hostname switch
!
enable secret 5 $1$mERr$G6rRG3ftDWE7LtIkBa5Fx.
```

- o **Password Encryption** = In the previous lab, we encrypted the enable password. As in other labs, however, there are many other passwords on network devices which would still be legible such as the console or telnet passwords. There is a method to encrypt all passwords on a network device. The process is as follows:
  - ☐ 1ST_Sw# Config t
  - ☐ 1ST_Sw (Config)# service password-encryption
  - ☐ 1ST_Sw (Config)# end
  - ☐ 1ST_Sw# sh run (Now all passwords will appear as a random string of letters and numbers).

VLAN Configuration (Virtual Local Area Network):

Configuring VLANs is a very good idea in order to reduce network congestion as well as created security areas. Vlan Names and numbers are case-sensitive so great care must be taken when attempting to create matching VLANs on different Switches.

- **2PC-to-Switch VLANs** = Virtual Local Area Networks are created and managed by switch software. Essentially, sections of memory are used to allow communications between specific computers. Multiple sections can be created which are not allowed to communicate to other sections. This creates a boundary of security between specific groups of computers.

- The following are the commands required to configure a VLAN on a switch. Before starting, give two PC the following network settings using "netsh" on the command line:

o Computer "A":
  □ IP Address = 172.16.20.10
  □ Subnet Mask = 255.255.255.0
  □ Default Gateway = 172.16.20.1
  □ Interface = fa0/5
o Computer "B":
  □ IP Address = 172.16.20.20
  □ Subnet Mask = 255.255.255.0
  □ Default Gateway = 172.16.20.1
  □ Interface = fa0/10
o Go to computer "A" and open the CLI.
o Ping computer "B" two times (The first ping may be 60% but the remainder will be 100%).
o Now we will create a VLAN with the following commands:
  □ 1ST_Sw# Config t
  □ 1ST_Sw (Config)# vlan 20 (Gives the vlan a number reference)
  □ 1ST_Sw (Config-vlan)# name staff (Optional to identify purpose).
  □ 1ST_Sw (Config-vlan)# end

```
1ST_Sw#conf t
Enter configuration commands, one per line.  End with CNTL/Z.
1ST_Sw(config)#vlan 20
1ST_Sw(config-vlan)#name staff
1ST_Sw(config-vlan)#end
1ST_Sw#
%SYS-5-CONFIG_I: Configured from console by console
```

☐ 1ST_Sw# sh vlan (Displays all vlans and associated interfaces).

```
1ST_Sw#sh vlan

VLAN Name                             Status      Ports
---- -------------------------------- ----------  ------------------------------
1    default                          active      Fa0/1, Fa0/2, Fa0/3, Fa
                                                  Fa0/5, Fa0/6, Fa0/7, Fa
                                                  Fa0/9, Fa0/10, Fa0/11,
                                                  Fa0/13, Fa0/14, Fa0/15,
                                                  Fa0/17, Fa0/18, Fa0/19,
                                                  Fa0/21, Fa0/22, Fa0/23,
                                                  Gig1/1, Gig1/2
20   staff                            active
1002 fddi-default                     act/unsup
1003 token-ring-default               act/unsup
1004 fddinet-default                  act/unsup
1005 trnet-default                    act/unsup
```

  o Now we will place one interface into VLAN 20:
      ☐ 1ST_Sw# Config t
      ☐ 1ST_Sw (Config)# int fa0/5
      ☐ 1ST_Sw (Config-if)# switchport access vlan 20
      ☐ 1ST_Sw (Config-if)# end
      ☐ 1ST_Sw# sh vlan (Shows interfaces in VLAN 20).

```
1ST_Sw#sh vlan

VLAN Name                             Status      Ports
---- -------------------------------- ----------  ------------------------------
1    default                          active      Fa0/1, Fa0/2,
                                                  Fa0/6, Fa0/7,
                                                  Fa0/11, Fa0/12
                                                  Fa0/15, Fa0/16
                                                  Fa0/19, Fa0/20
                                                  Fa0/23, Fa0/24
20   staff                            active      Fa0/5, Fa0/10
```

  o Go to computer "A" and open the CLI.
  o Ping computer "B" two times (The communication fails because they are not in a vlan).
  o Now we will place the other interface into VLAN 20:
      ☐ 1ST_Sw (Config)# int fa0/10
      ☐ 1ST_Sw (Config-if)# switchport access vlan 20

- □ 1ST_Sw (Config-if)# end
- □ 1ST_Sw# sh vlan (Shows interfaces in VLAN 20).
- o Go to computer "A" and open the CLI.
- o Ping computer "B" two times (The first ping may be 60% but the remainder will be 100%).

Creating a File Share Windows 10 (Non-Domain Client):

With this example, we will totally disable all security to make access easier. When you work on a computer in an office environment, the settings will be more customized. The following list is not all-inclusive and the associated videos are more detailed.

1) Make sure all firewalls are off.

Allow an app or feature through Windows Firewall

through the Internet or a network.

Change notification settings

Turn Windows Firewall on or off

Restore defaults

Advanced settings

Troubleshoot my network

Private networks

Networks at home or work where yc

Windows Firewall state:

Incoming connections:

Active private networks:

2) Make all the "Green" icons turn "Red".

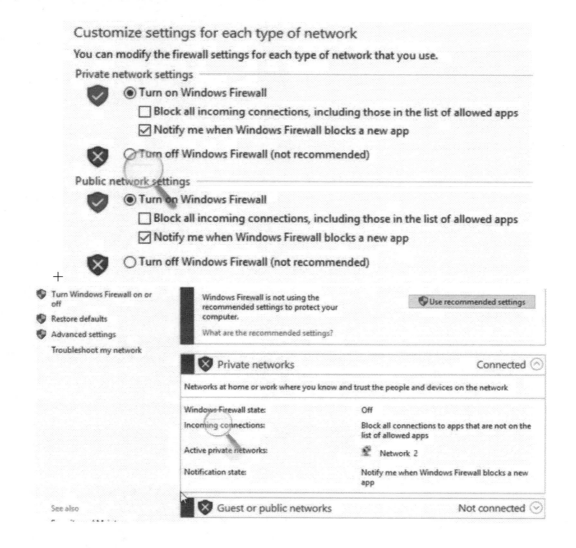

Customize settings for each type of network

You can modify the firewall settings for each type of network that you use.

Private network settings

◉ Turn on Windows Firewall

☐ Block all incoming connections, including those in the list of allowed apps

☑ Notify me when Windows Firewall blocks a new app

○ Turn off Windows Firewall (not recommended)

Public network settings

◉ Turn on Windows Firewall

☐ Block all incoming connections, including those in the list of allowed apps

☑ Notify me when Windows Firewall blocks a new app

○ Turn off Windows Firewall (not recommended)

Turn Windows Firewall on or off

Restore defaults

Advanced settings

Troubleshoot my network

Windows Firewall is not using the recommended settings to protect your computer.

Use recommended settings

What are the recommended settings?

Private networks   Connected

Networks at home or work where you know and trust the people and devices on the network

Windows Firewall state: Off

Incoming connections: Block all connections to apps that are not on the list of allowed apps

Active private networks: Network 2

Notification state: Notify me when Windows Firewall blocks a new app

See also

Guest or public networks   Not connected

3) Turn off "Password Protection".

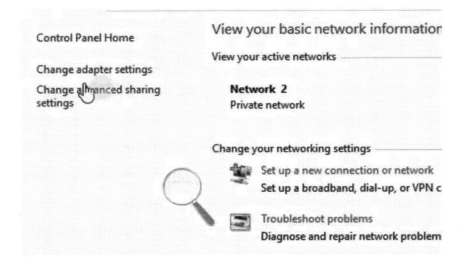

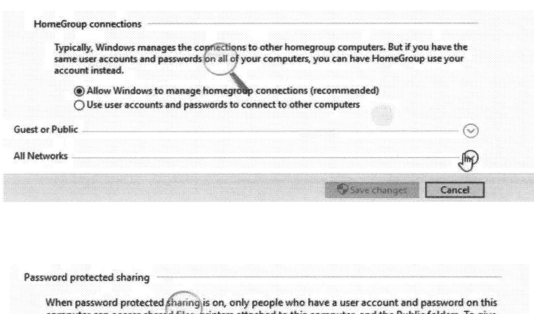

4) Assure you have the correct IP address and other computers can ping the IP address.

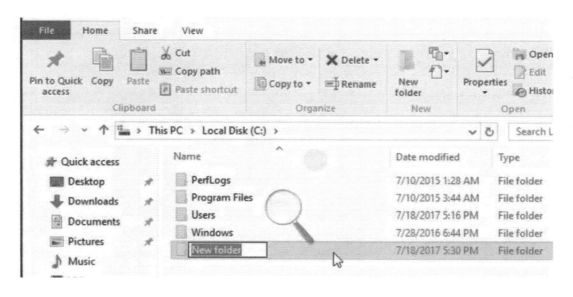

```
-local IPv6 Address . . . . . : fe80::40b:c878
 Address. . . . . . . . . . . : 10.10.41.76
et Mask . . . . . . . . . . . : 255.255.248.0

 Command Prompt

 Microsoft Windows [Version 10.0.14393]
 (c) 2016 Microsoft Corporation. All rights reserved.

 C:\Users\c308>ping 10.10.41.76

 Pinging 10.10.41.76 with 32 bytes of data:
 Reply from 10.10.41.76: bytes=32 time<1ms TTL=128
 Reply from 10.10.41.76: bytes=32 time<1ms TTL=128
 Reply from 10.10.41.76: bytes=32 time<1ms TTL=128
 Reply from 10.10.41.76: bytes=32 time<   TTL=128

 Ping statistics for 10.10.41.76:
     Packets: Sent = 4, Received = 4, Lost =   (0% loss),
 Approximate round trip times in milli-seconds:
     Minimum = 0ms, Maximum = 0ms, Average = 0ms
```

5) Create needed folders inside of "C" drive (Some of these folders are used for other exercise).

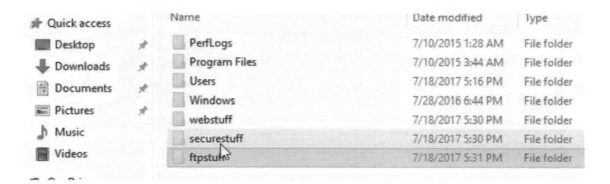

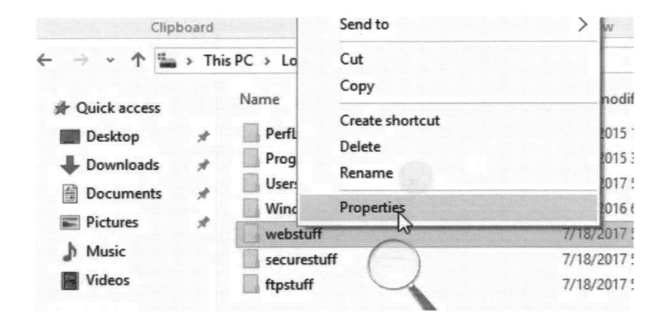

6) Configure "Share" permissions on each folder.

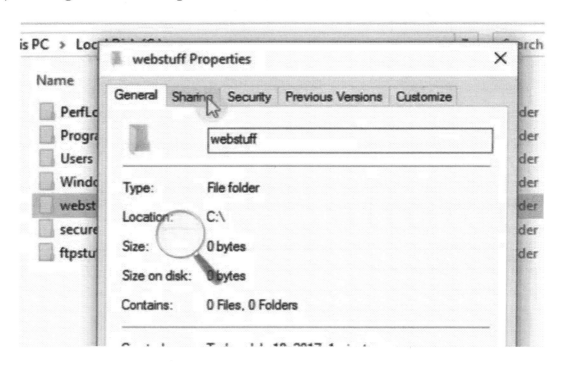

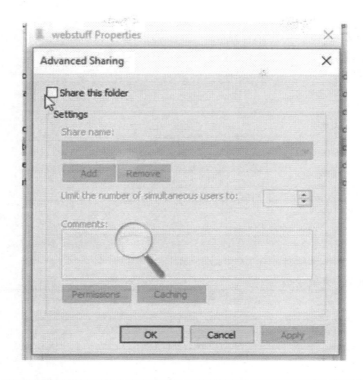

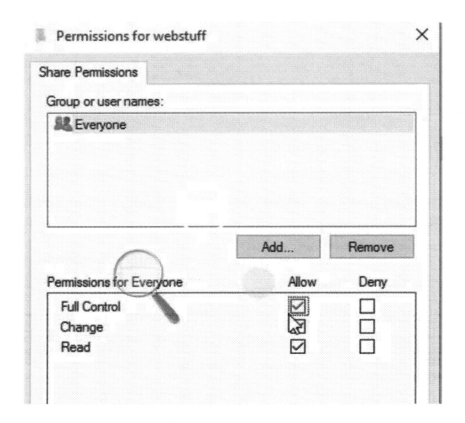

7) Configure "Security" permissions on each folder.

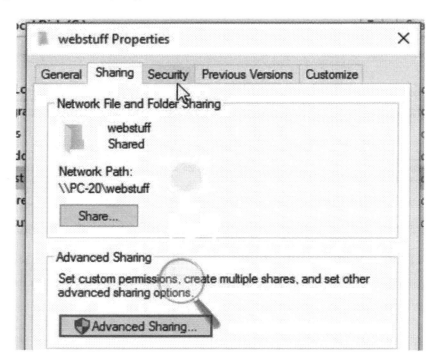

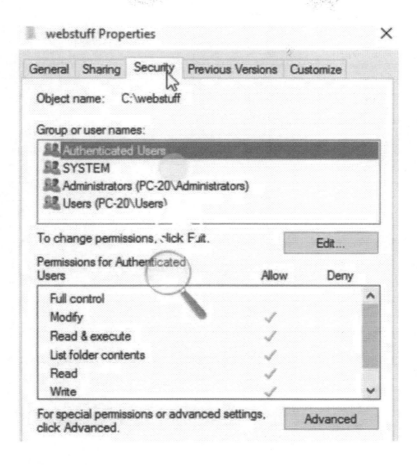

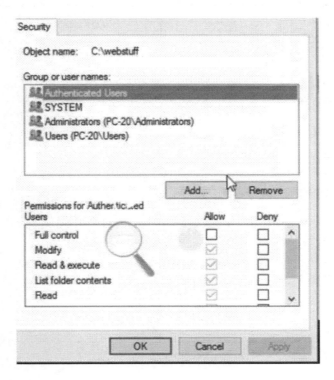

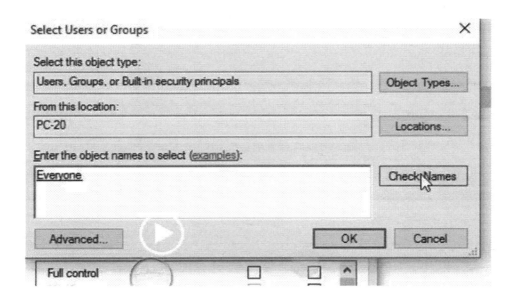

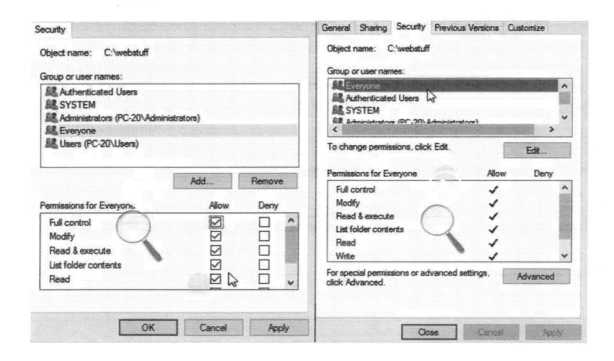

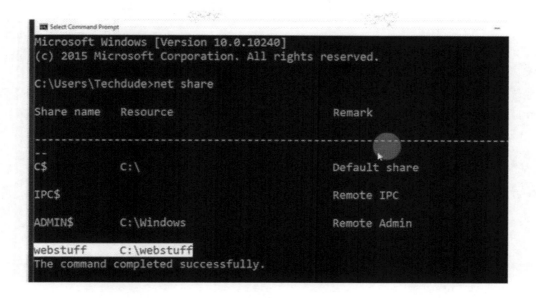

```
Microsoft Windows [Version 10.0.10240]
(c) 2015 Microsoft Corporation. All rights reserved.

C:\Users\Techdude>net share

Share name     Resource                        Remark

--
C$             C:\                             Default share

IPC$                                           Remote IPC

ADMIN$         C:\Windows                      Remote Admin

webstuff       C:\webstuff
The command completed successfully.
```

```
Ethernet adapter Ethernet:

   Connection-specific DNS Suffix  . : ccp.edu
   Link-local IPv6 Address . . . . . : fe80::40b:c878:c
   IPv4 Address. . . . . . . . . . . : 10.10.41.76
   Subnet Mask . . . . . . . . . . . : 255.255.248.0
```

8) Check to assure that the folders are shared two ways:
  ➤ **"Net Share" utility:**

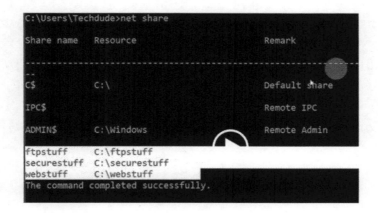

```
C:\Users\Techdude>net share

Share name     Resource                        Remark

--
C$             C:\                             Default share

IPC$                                           Remote IPC

ADMIN$         C:\Windows                      Remote Admin

ftpstuff       C:\ftpstuff
securestuff    C:\securestuff
webstuff       C:\webstuff
The command completed successfully.
```

> ➤ "UNC" method:

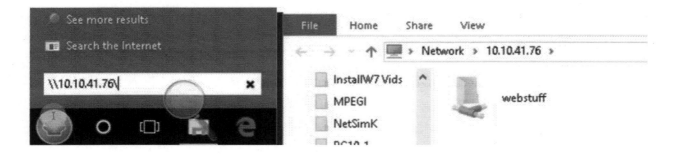

9) **Now anyone on the network who can "ping" your computer will be able to access any files you place in the shared folders.**

Installing Internet Information Services (Windows 10 or Server 2012):

With this example, we will illustrate the process of enabling services on a Windows Operating system to support the function of allowing the computer to be a Web Server or FTP Server. Many other features are available after this installation such as Security Server, E-mail and Streaming Video (None of which will be performed in this textbook, but still important to mention). The following list is not all-inclusive and the associated videos are more detailed.

1) **Access "Control Panel" under "Apps" and "Windows Systems".**

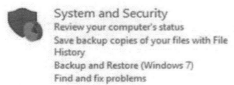

Adjust your computer's settings

View by: Category ▼

System and Security
Review your computer's status
Save backup copies of your files with File History
Backup and Restore (Windows 7)
Find and fix problems

Network and Internet
View network status and tasks
Choose homegroup and sharing options

Hardware and Sound
View devices and printers
Add a device

Programs
Uninstall a program

User Accounts
🛡 Change account type

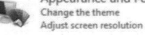
Appearance and Personalization
Change the theme
Adjust screen resolution

Clock, Language, and Region
Add a language
Change input methods
Change date, time, or number formats

Ease of Access
Let Windows suggest settings
Optimize visual display

2) **Click on "Programs" then "Turn Windows Features on and off".**

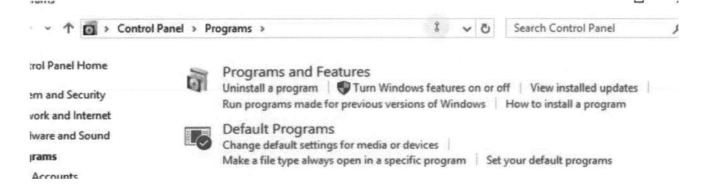

:rol Panel Home

:m and Security

vork and Internet

lware and Sound

jrams

Accounts

Programs and Features
Uninstall a program | 🛡 Turn Windows features on or off | View installed updates |
Run programs made for previous versions of Windows | How to install a program

Default Programs
Change default settings for media or devices |
Make a file type always open in a specific program | Set your default programs

3) **Select the following options under "Internet Information Services:**
   ➢ **FTP Server** (All Services)
   ➢ **Web Management Tools** (All Services)
   ➢ **World Wide Web Services** = All services EXCEPT "Application
      Development Features" and "Windows Authentication" inside of
      "Security".
   ➢ **Internet Information Services Hostable Web Core.**

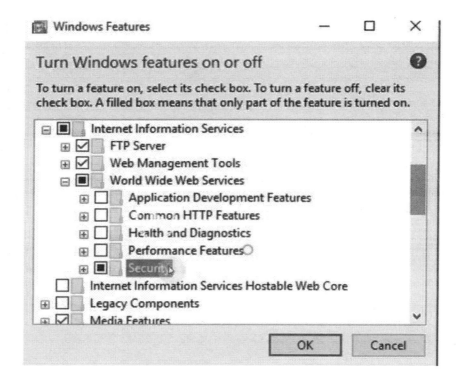

Windows completed the requested changes.

4) **Now access the control MMC for IIS under "Windows Administrative Tools" or search for IIS.**

5) **Use the IIS vs. 7 MMC (It is the one "WITHOUT A NUMBER" (Microsoft idea! LOL))**

6) **Expand the IIS snap-ins until you view options for the "Default Web Site".**

7) **Access the default website from any computer that can "Ping" this computer to see if the default IIS website is viewable.**

```
Windows IP Configuration


Ethernet adapter Ethernet:

   Connection-specific DNS Suffix  . : ccp.edu
   Link-local IPv6 Address . . . . . : fe80::40b:c878:c7c0:c90f%6
   IPv4 Address. . . . . . . . . . . : 10.10.41.76
   Subnet Mask . . . . . . . . . . . : 255.255.248.0
   Default Gateway . . . . . . . . . : 10.10.40.1
```

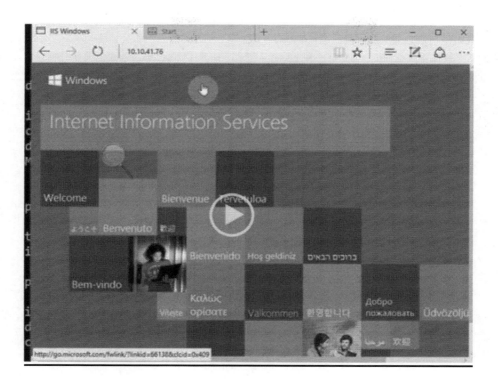

Creating an Open Website (Windows 10 or Server 2012):

In this illustration, we will review the process used to create directories to hold webpage files and assure they can be accessed from other computers (This step done in previous exercises). Assure IIS has been installed on the computer and place a shortcut on the desktop as well (This step done in previous exercises). In addition, please review the associated videos for greater detail.

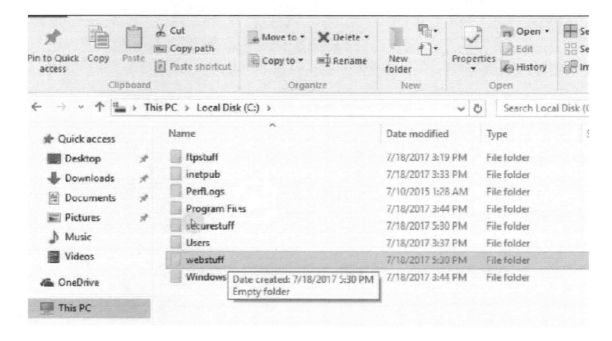

1) **Create the open webpage using a word processor and save it with the name "index.htm" as a "Complete Website" in the "opensite" directory.**

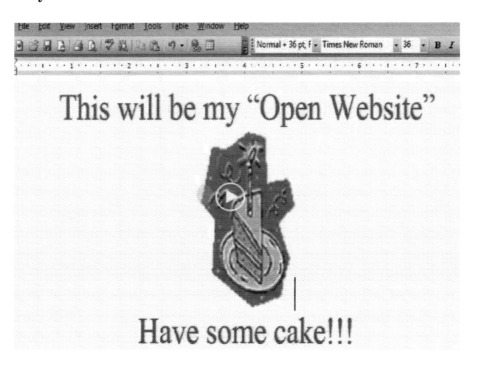

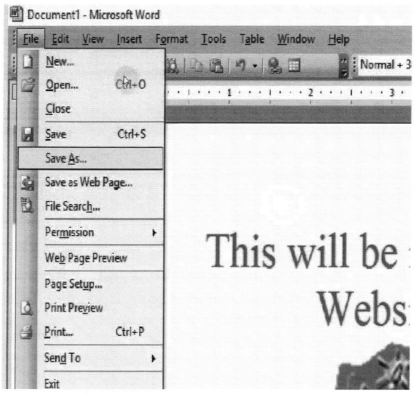

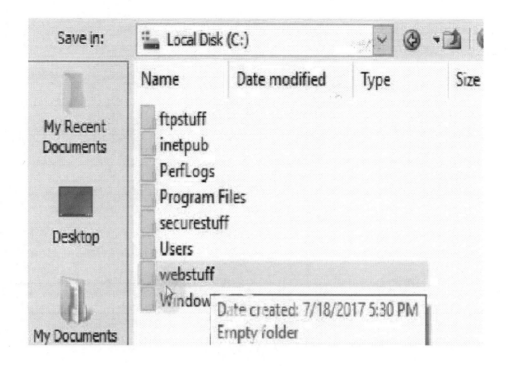

2) Check the directory and look for the "index file".

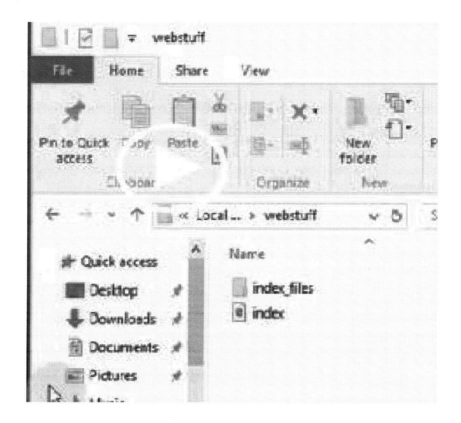

3) Configure IIS to make this webpage available from the server.
4) Access the IIS MMC, disable the "Default-Website" by selecting the "default web site", and click the "stop" button.

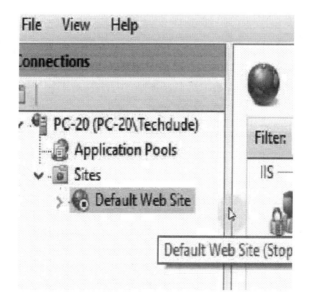

5) Create the website in IIS by right-clicking the "Sites" snap-in and select "Add Website".

6) Complete fields with the following information:
 - ➢ Site Name
 - ➢ Physical Path (Where web page files exist)
 - ➢ Type (Open Website-http)
 - ➢ IP address - Select desired IP address if more than one exists.

7) **Now test your website using the servers IP address on the server's browser.**

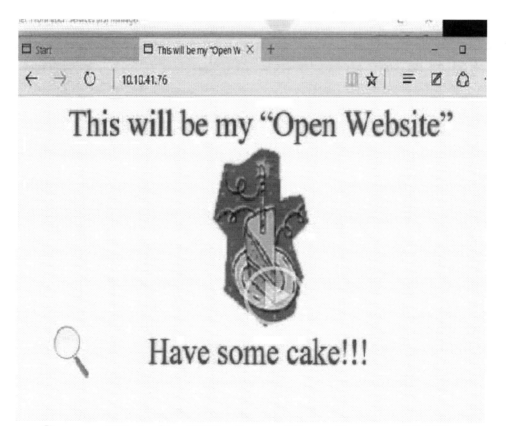

Creating a Secure Website (Windows 10 or Server 2012):

The following will display a process used daily by network administrators and computer technicians. We will illustrate a process to activate and host a Secure

Website on either Windows 10 or Server 2012. The following list is not all-inclusive and the associated videos are more detailed.

In order to host a website on a server it is necessary to create a shared directory to hold webpage files and assure they can be accessed from other computers (This step done in a previous exercise). Assure IIS has been installed on the computer and place a shortcut on the desktop as well (This step done in a previous exercise).

1) **Create the secure webpage using a word processor and save it with the name "index.htm" as a "Complete Website" in a shared directory as was done in the "open website" exercise.**
2) **Check the directory and look for the "index file".**
3) **Configure IIS to make this a secure webpage available from the server. Start by opening IIS and click on the name of the server.**

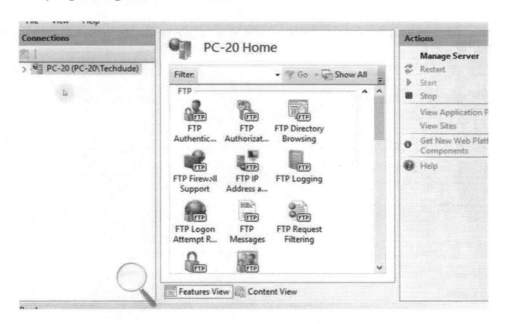

4) **Access the IIS MMC, disable the "Default-Website" by selecting the "default web site", and click the "stop" button. Create a "SSL Certificate" for the website by accessing the "Webserver Home" Pane, then locate "Server Certificates" and double-click it.**

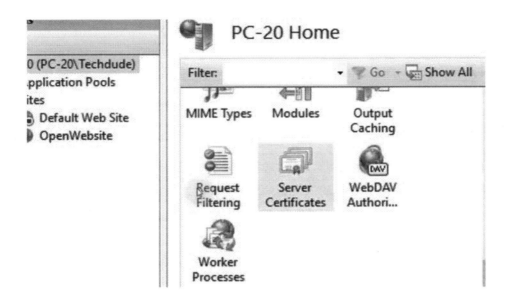

5) Go to the right-side, double-click the "Create Self-Signed Certificate", and give it an easy name.

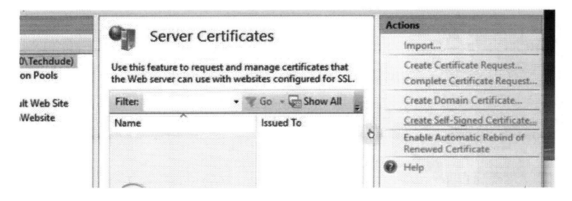

6) Click "OK" and it appears in the list of available certificates.

7) Create the website in IIS by taking the mouse and "Right-Click" the "Sites" snap-in and select "Add Website".

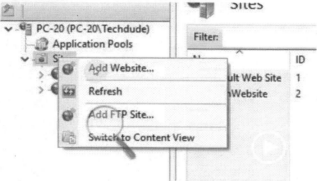

8) Complete the fields with the following required information:
9) Site Name
   - ➢ Physical Path (Where web page files exist)
   - ➢ Type (Secure Website-https)
   - ➢ IP address - Select desired IP address if more than one exists.
   - ➢ Select the port number to be used.
   - ➢ Select the name of the certificate to be used and click "OK".

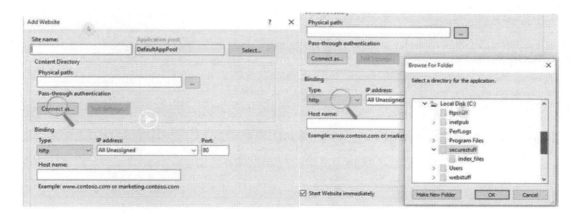

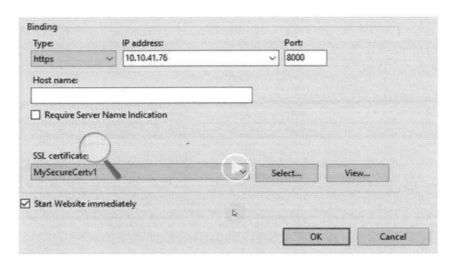

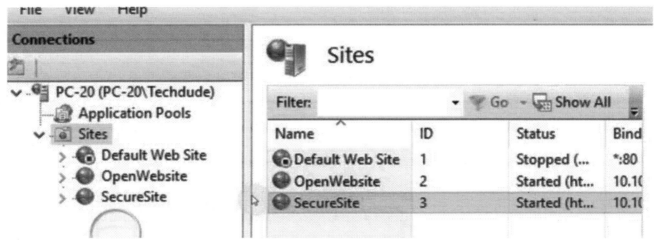

10) Now test your secure website using the "https" and the servers IP address with the websites "Port Number" proceeded by a colon (:) on the server's browser.

11) Just as before, depending on your browser, you will get a message indicating there is a "certificate Problem".

There is a problem with this website's security certificate

We recommend that you close this webpage and do not continue to this website.

The security certificate for this site doesn't match the site's web address and may indicate an attempt to fool you or intercept any data you send to the server.

Go to my homepage instead

Continue to this webpage (not recommended)

12) This means that the certificate you created is not presently on the browser you are using. This is OK. You can install it later. Look for options that allow you to "Continue to the site anyway".

13) When the "Secure Site" index page loads, attempt to access the webpage from any other computer that can ping the server.

Configuring FQDN Access (Windows 10 or Server 2012):

With this example, we will illustrate the process of enabling a file, which enables the location of network and internet resources using a "Domain Name" or "Fully Qualified Domain Name" on a Windows Operating System computer. The following list is not all-inclusive and the associated videos are more detailed. You must be logged in as "Administrator" to perform the actions required for this task. After creating a website, you will have to access the "host file". The path is as follows: "C:\Windows\System32\Drivers\etc>":

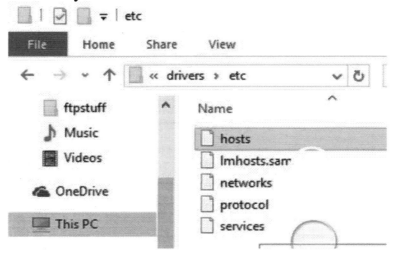

1) Copy the "Hosts" file to make a backup (Just in case we make a mistake). After copying, edit the file by opening it in "notepad".

2) **Modify one of the lines by inserting your webservers IP address and the domain name used to locate the website.**

```
# entry should be kept on an individual line. The IP address should
# be placed in the first column followed by the corresponding host name.
# The IP address and the host name should be separated by at least one
# space.
#
# Additionally, comments (such as these) may be inserted on individual
# lines or following the machine name denoted by a '#' symbol.
#
# For example:
#
#      102.54.94.97     rhino.acme.com          # source server
#       38.25.63.10     x.acme.com              # x client host

# localhost name resolution is handled within DNS itself.
#       127.0.0.1       localhost
#       ::1             localhost
```

3) **Remove the first "#" symbol and keep the columns lined up.**

```
        10.10.41.76      cooldude.com           # source server
#       38.25.63.10      x.acme.com             # x client host
```

4) **After saving the file, sign out and sign-in as a normal user ("CCP1" or "CCP2"). Open a browser and go to the domain name you setup in the "Hosts" file. Your website should now appear.**

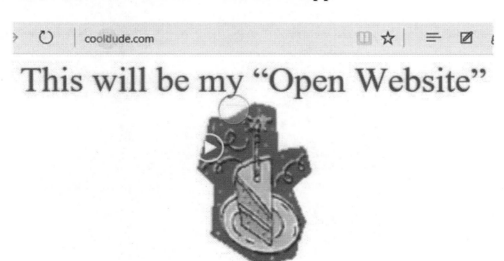

Creating an FTP Site (Windows 10 or Server 2012):

Assure IIS has been installed on the computer (This step done in a previous exercise). Create a shared directory to store FTP files and assure it can be accessed from other computers (This step done in a previous exercise). The following steps are not all-inclusive. More detailed instructions are displayed in the videos associated with this exercise.

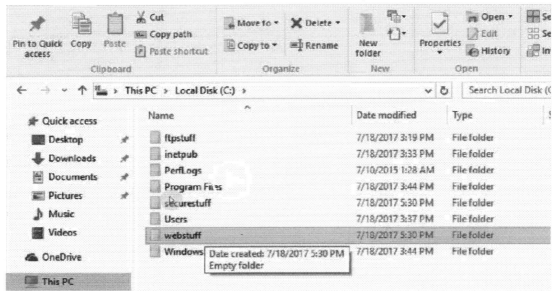

1) **Place some random files within the directory that will be used for FTP (Just to test later).**

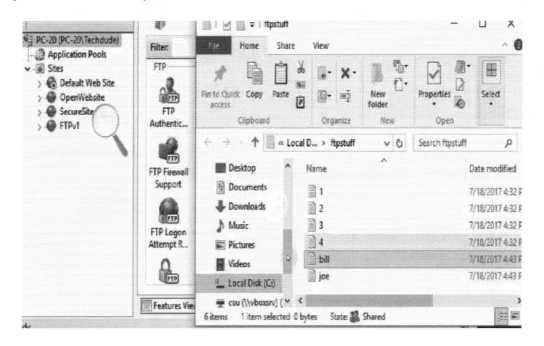

2) Configure IIS to make this FTP Site available from the server by creating the FTP site in IIS by using the mouse to "Right-Click" the "Sites" snap-in and select "Add FTP site". Complete with the following:

> ➤ **-Site Name**
> ➤ **-Physical Path (Where FTP folder exists)**
> ➤ **-IP address - Select desired IP address if more than one exists.**

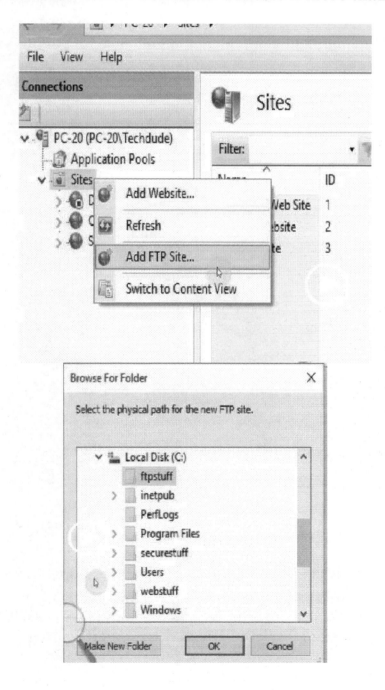

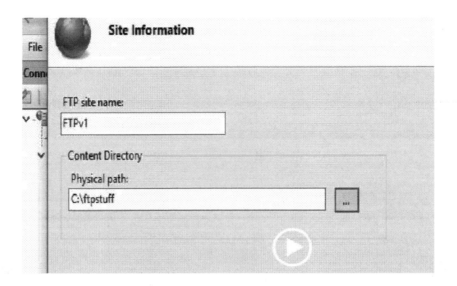

3) Assure check mark is in "Start FTP site automatically", then select "No SSL" and "Next".

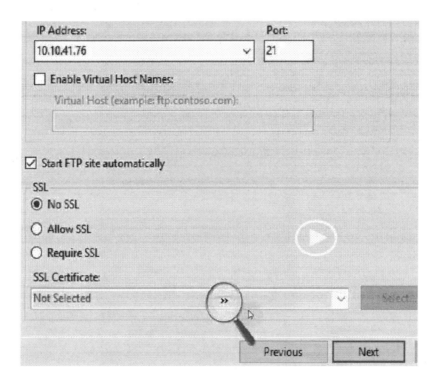

4) Place check marks in both "Anonymous" and "Basic" under "Authentication".
5) Under "Authorization-Allow Access to:" select "All users".
6) Under "Permissions" select "Read" and "Write" then click "Finish".

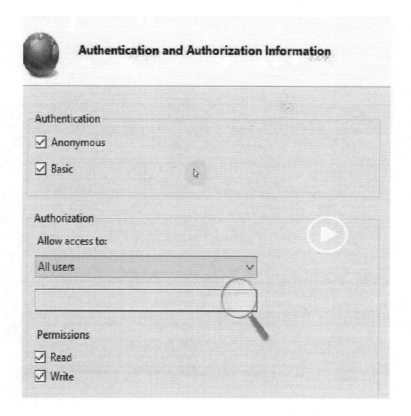

Authentication and Authorization Information

Authentication
- ☑ Anonymous
- ☑ Basic

Authorization
Allow access to:

| All users | ⌄ |

Permissions
- ☑ Read
- ☑ Write

7) **The new FTP site should now list in IIS. I would suggest restarting all IIS services.**

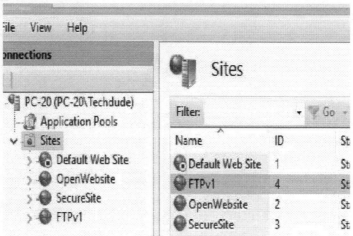

8) Go to another computer that can "ping" the ftp server and attempt to create directories, rename files, upload files, download files, etc.

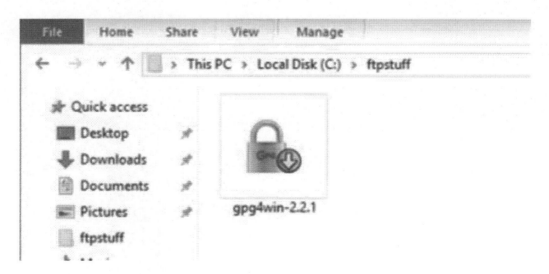

Configuring PKI for Users (Windows 7 or Windows 10):

*Notes: You must be logged in as "Administrator" to perform the actions required for this task. The following is an example of using a security method combining "encryption" and a "Public Key Infrastructure". The listed steps are not all-inclusive. More detailed instructions are displayed in the videos associated with this exercise.

1) **You must install encryption software that can create Public and Private Keys such as "Gpg4Win" which will enable a program called "Kleopatra".**

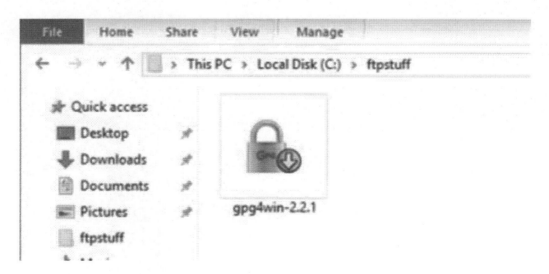

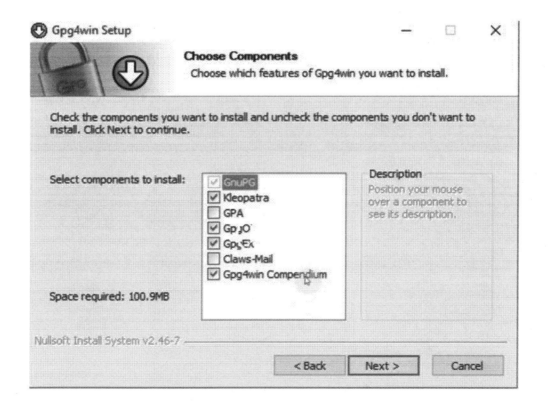

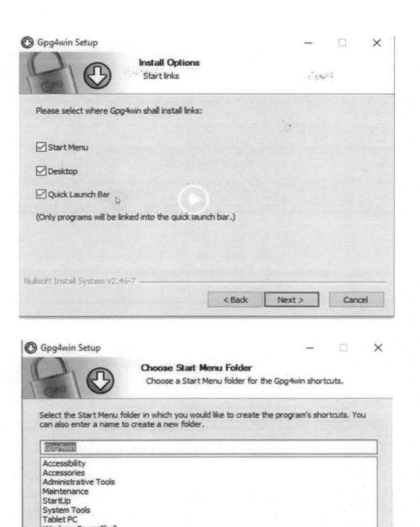

2) **After Installing "GPG4Win" you will notice a new icon called "Kleopatra".**

3) **Use this interface to create a PKI and store it to a location other users can use to install it into their version of "Kleopatra".**

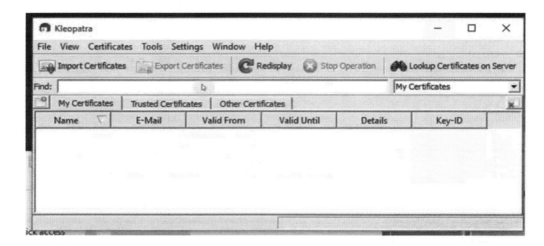

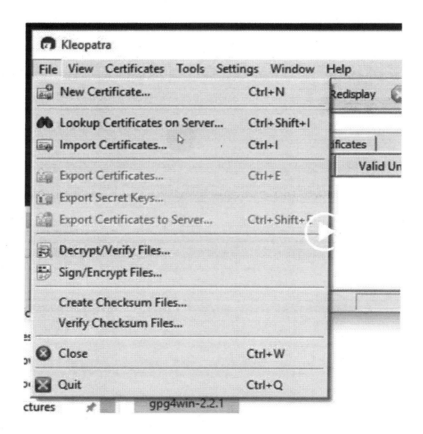

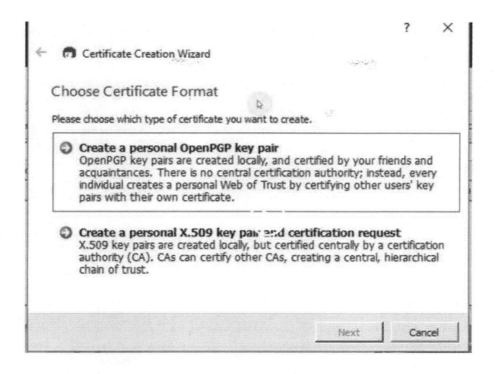

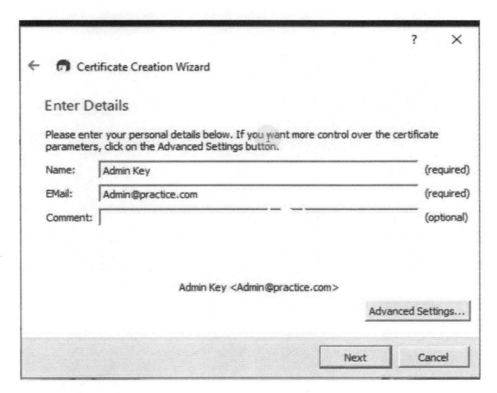

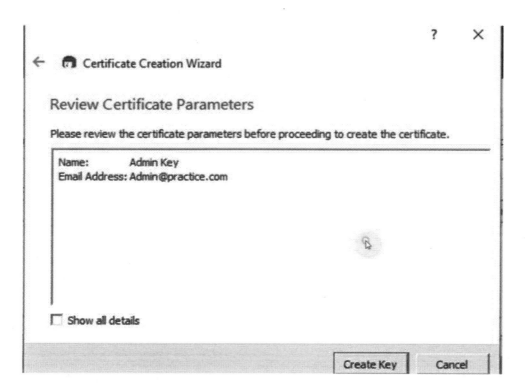

Creating Key...

Your key is being created.

The process of creating a key requires large amounts of random numbers. To foster this process, you can use the entry field below to enter some gibberish. The text itself does not matter - only the inter-character timing. You can also move this window around with your mouse, or sta...

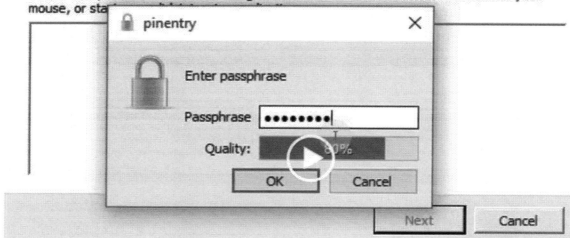

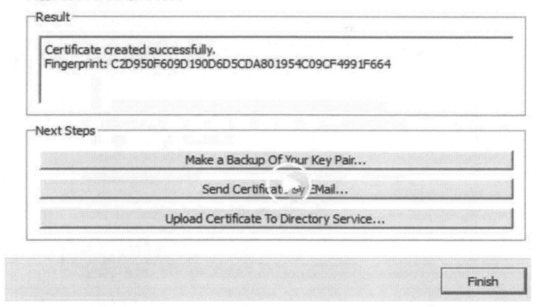

Key Pair Successfully Created

Your new key pair was created successfully. Please find details on the result and some suggested next steps below.

Result

Certificate created successfully.
Fingerprint: C2D950F609D190D6D5CDA801954C09CF4991F664

Next Steps

Make a Backup Of Your Key Pair...

Send Certificate by Mail...

Upload Certificate To Directory Service...

Finish

4) **Create a document, encrypt it and store the encrypted version in the network drive.**

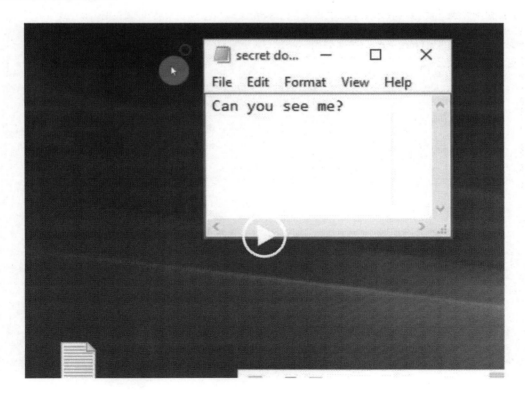

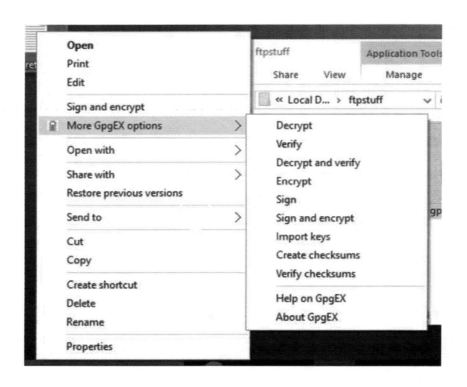

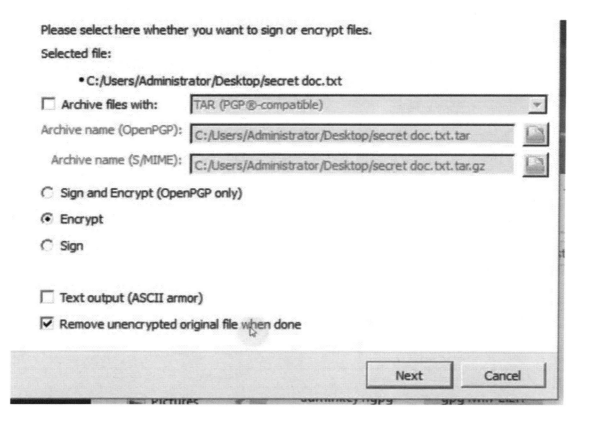

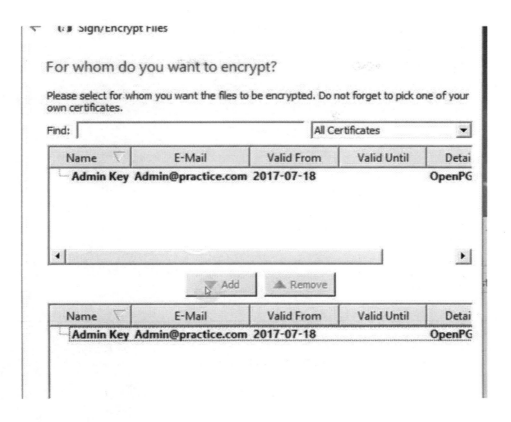

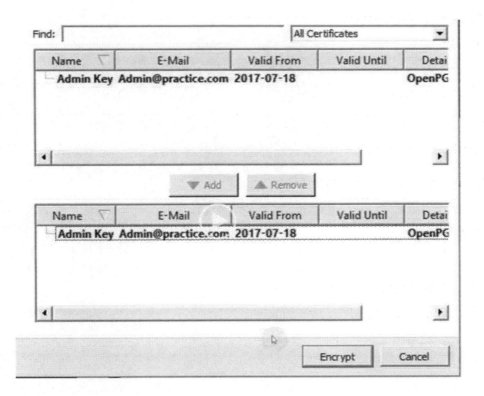

OpenPGP: All operations completed.

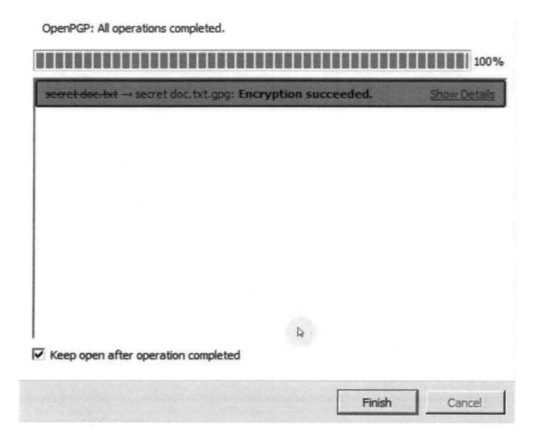

secret doc.txt → secret doc.txt.gpg: **Encryption succeeded.** Show Details

☑ Keep open after operation completed

Finish   Cancel

5) **Sign-out and login as another user. You notice that the other user has "Kleopatra" but it has no keys. Copy both the "PKI" and the "Encrypted Document" to the desktop.**

6) **Try to open the "encrypted document" and it fails. If you select "Notepad" to open it, the characters are illegible.**

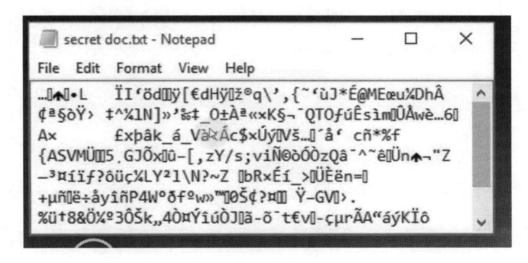

7) **The user requires the correct "public key" in order to "unscramble" the message in the encrypted file. Add the key to the user's account.**

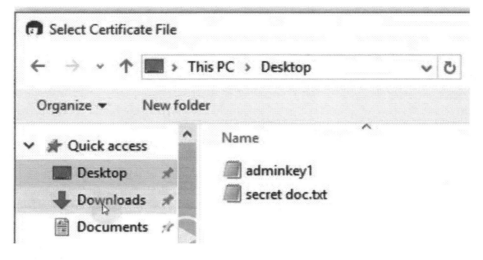

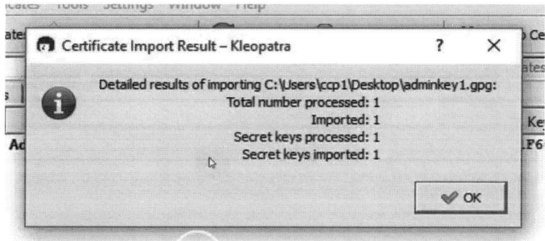

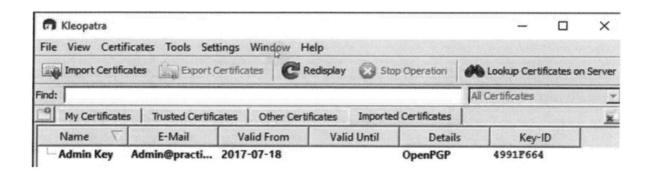

8) Decrypt the encrypted file using the appropriate key and passphrase.

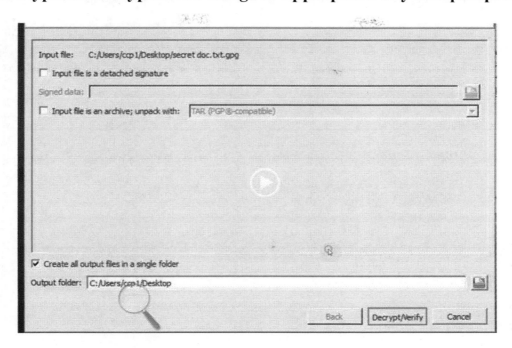

9) The decryption will require you to input the passcode the original owner of the key used.

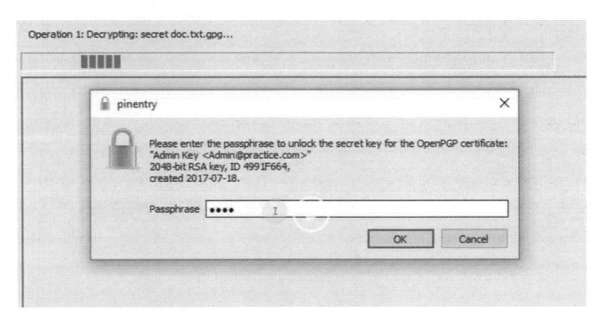

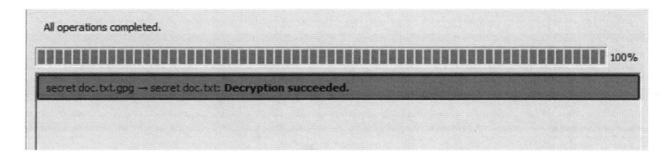

All operations completed.

100%

secret doc.txt.gpg → secret doc.txt: **Decryption succeeded.**

10)   **Now this user will be able to read the file.**

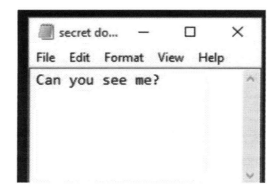

Configuring Steganography for Users (Windows 7 or Windows 10):

*Notes: You must be logged in as "Administrator" to perform the actions required for this task. The following is an example of using a method of hiding messages in photos. The listed steps are not all-inclusive. More detail instructions are displayed in the videos associated with this exercise. You must install Steganography software to hide and reveal messages in graphic files such as program called "Quick Stego".

1) **You must install encryption software that can create Public and Private Keys such as "Gpg4Win" which will enable a program called "Kleopatra".**

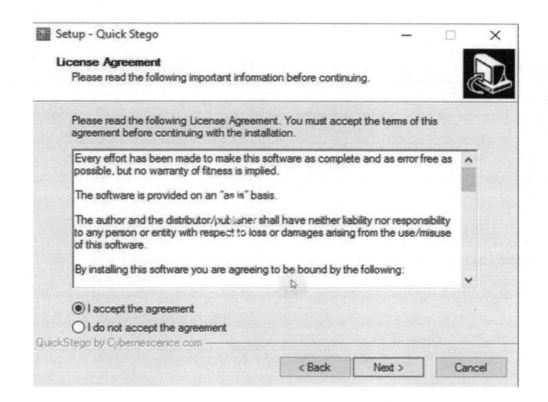

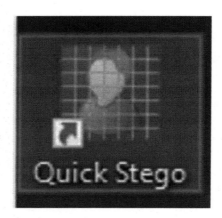

2) **After installing "Quick Stego". Open the application and view the interface. Here you can open photos and view or insert hidden messages.**

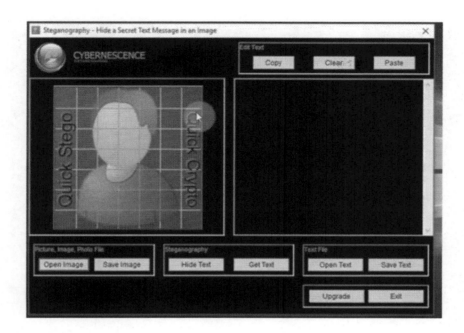

3) Below, we have inserted a hidden message.

4) View the picture in a graphic program. No message can be seen. If any other user has a copy of "Quick Stego" the message will display.

Configuring a POP Client (Windows 7 or Windows 10):

*Notes: The following is an example of using a method configuring an e-mail client to interact with an e-mail server. The listed steps are not all-inclusive. More detailed instructions are displayed in the videos associated with this exercise. We will use two clients. This project requires firewalls, shares and password protection to be disabled for full and total access to all computers. We will use the POP client called "Microsoft Outlook". We will connect the clients to the server by using an SMTP/POP based E-Mail Server software called "Icewarp Merak Mail".

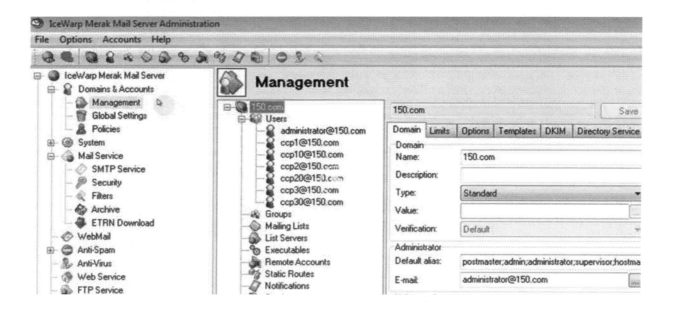

The E-mail server software has already been installed. In addition, users have already been created and are part of "150.COM". We will use "CCP1" and "CCP2" for our tests. All of their passwords are "Password1". In order to connect client software to the E-mail Server, it will be necessary to launch the client as each user, configure the client for the user, and connect each client's account to the e-mail server.

1) **We will start by connecting a user (CCP1) on one of the computers we are using. Login as "CCP1". Launch Outlook and continue with "Next". Select "Yes" to connect to an E-mail Server.**

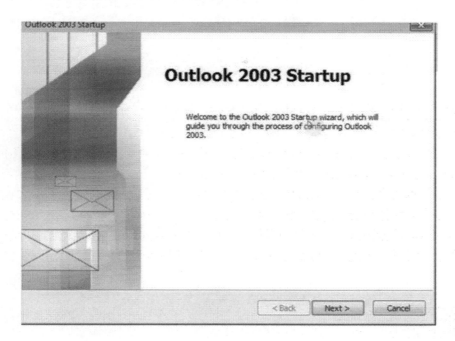

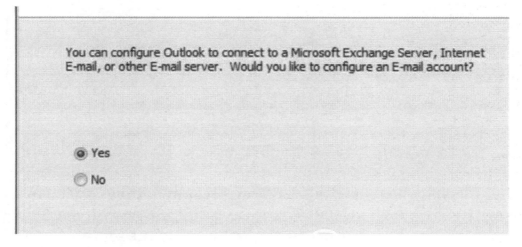

2) Select "POP3" for our exercise.

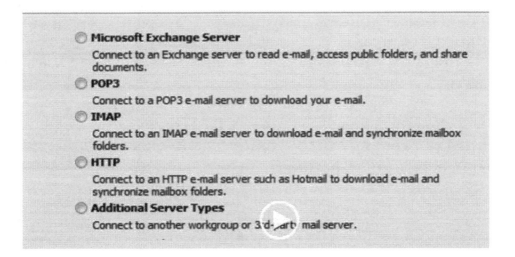

3) Complete the sections a displayed. In our exercise, we will use a single server's IP address for both POP3 and SMTP.

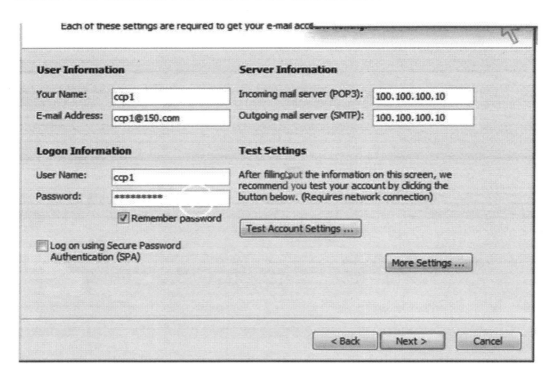

4) After placing all settings, click "Test Account Settings". You must get all GREEN Checkmarks. If not, the e-mail transfer will not work. If you get errors, try the password again and pinging the server.

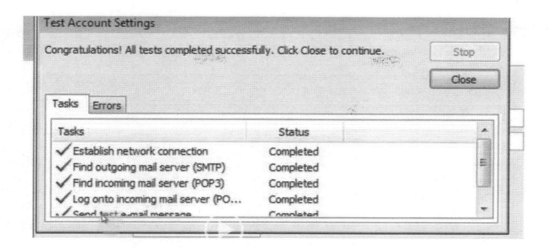

5) After viewing all green checkmarks. Continue and select "OK" for the user customization.

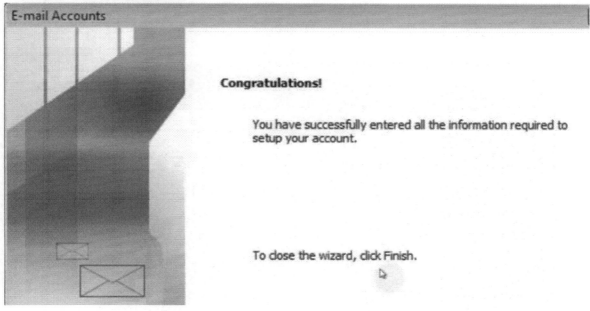

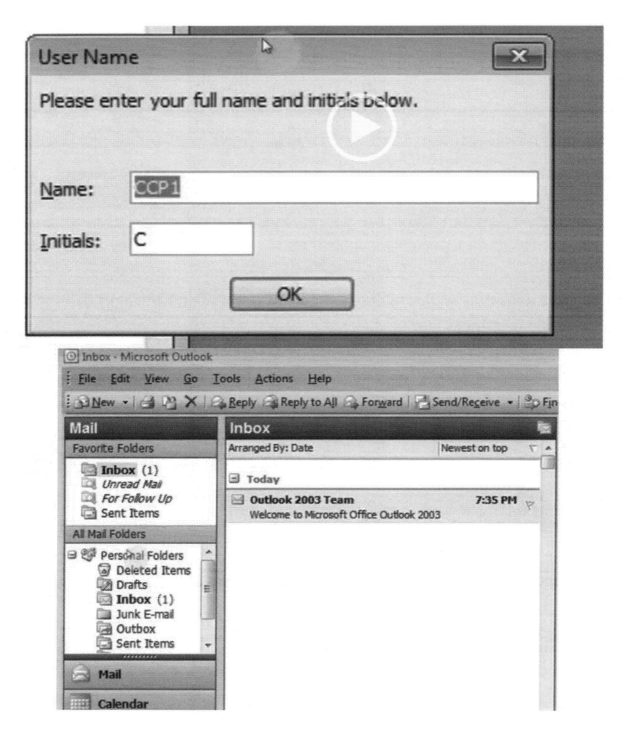

6) **Now let's test the account by sending a piece of e-mail to ourselves. Create the e-mail, then hit "Send". After you click "Send", you must also select "Send and Receive" to actually get the e-mail.**

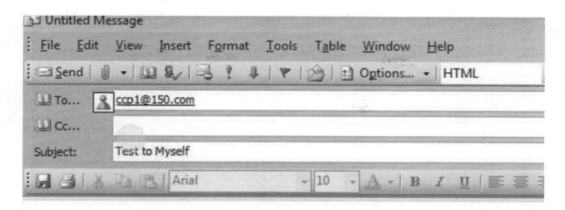

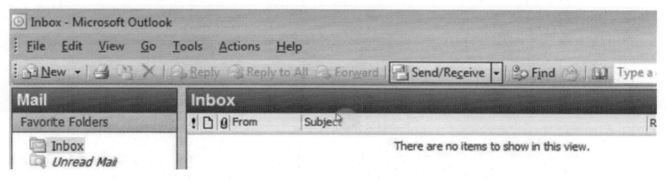

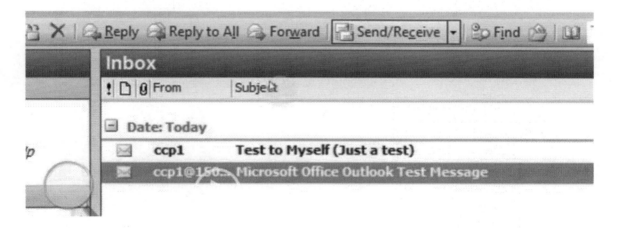

7) **To make the exercise more "real", we will make the client check for new e-mail and send created e-mail when we close out the software. You must further customize the accounts with the following steps:**

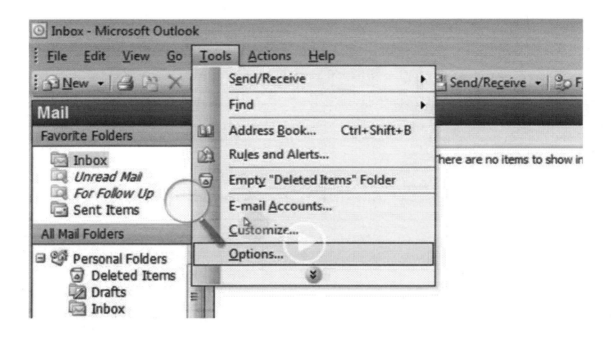

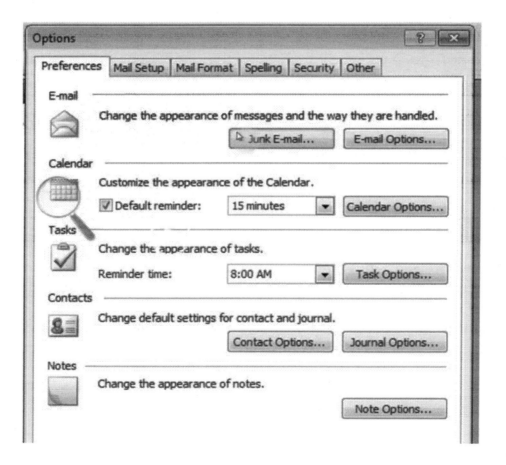

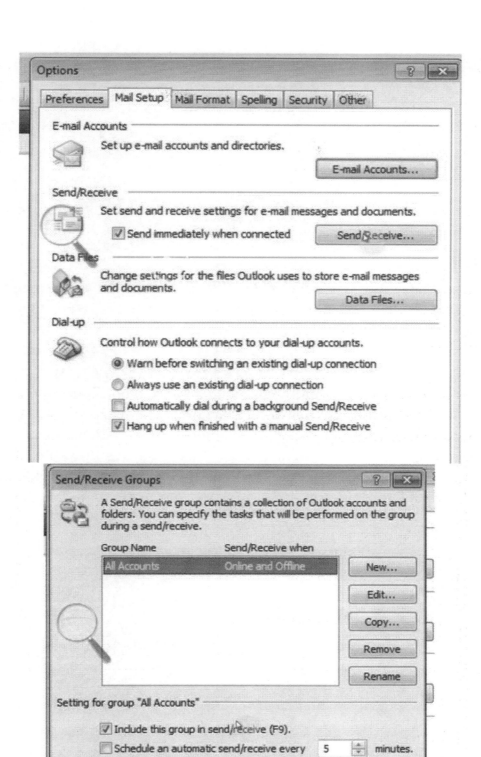

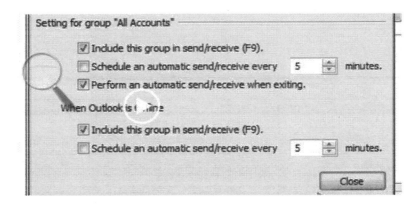

8) **Now, anytime a user clicks "Send" the mail will wait in queue until the user logs out of Outlook. Upon exiting, all mail the user clicked and approved to send will then be transmitted.**

Configuring a VoIP Client (Windows 7 or Windows 10):

*Notes: The following is an example of using a method configuring an Telephone Server Software with a Telephone user application. The listed steps are not all-inclusive. More detailed instructions are displayed in the videos associated with this exercise. We will use two clients. This project requires firewalls, shares and password protection to be disabled for full and total access to all computers (Completed in previous exercises). We will use the VoIP client called "3CXPhone" and two clients. The 3CXPhoneSystem server software has already been installed. The controls for the system are accessed via using "All Programs".

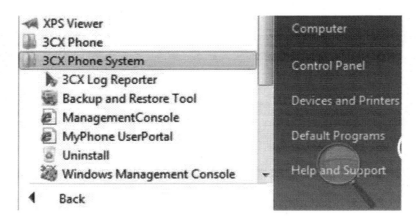

Presently, we are logged in as a CCP1 without higher rights. 3CXPhoneSystem will require us to insert the "Administrators" password of "Password1" to give us access.

1) Login with "administrator" and "Password1".

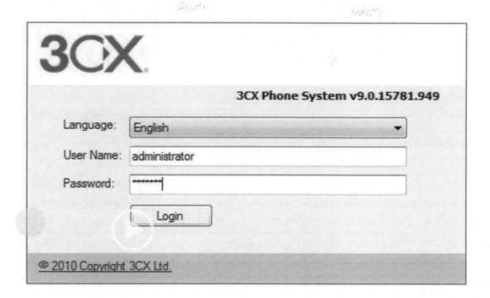

2) All the "Red Dots" are phone user accounts that have already been created on the system. Presently, we are logged in as a CCP1 without higher rights. 3CXPhoneSystem will require us to insert the "Administrators" password of "Password1" to give us access. All the "Red Dots" are phone user accounts that have already been created on the system.

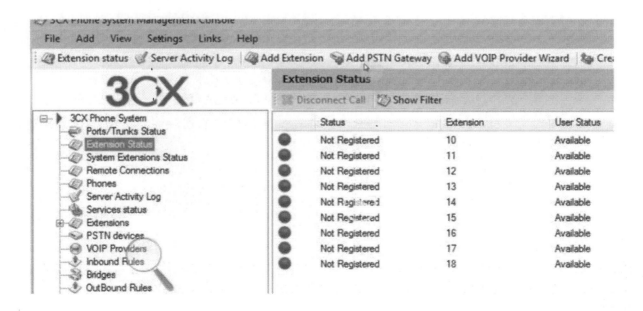

3) We will use "CCP1" and "CCP2" for our tests. All of their passwords are "Password1" for Windows, but they have "Unique" passwords for the VoIP System. You can access each user's passwords and account settings by double-clicking their extensions. To see the password, click the "ellipses" next to it.

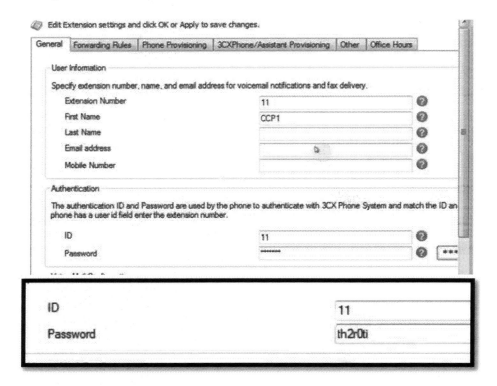

4) In order to connect client software to the 3CXPhoneSystem Server, it will be necessary to launch the client as each user, configure the client for the user, and connect each client's account to the VoIP server using its IP address. We will start by connecting a user (CCP1) to the 3CXPhoneSystem Server. It is fine to have users on the computer that is running the VoIP server software. Launch 3CXPhone and continue with "Create Profile" and "New".

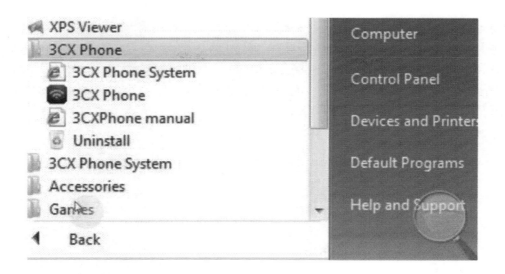

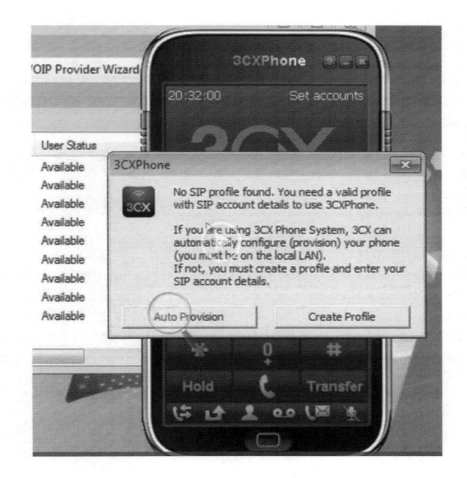

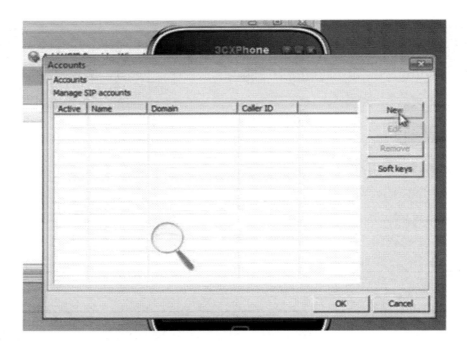

5) Here we will insert the username, ID, Extension and Password for the user.

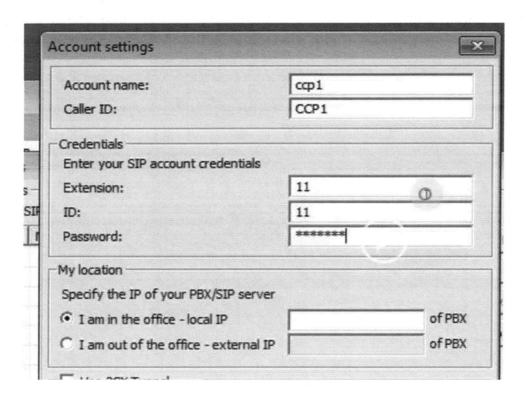

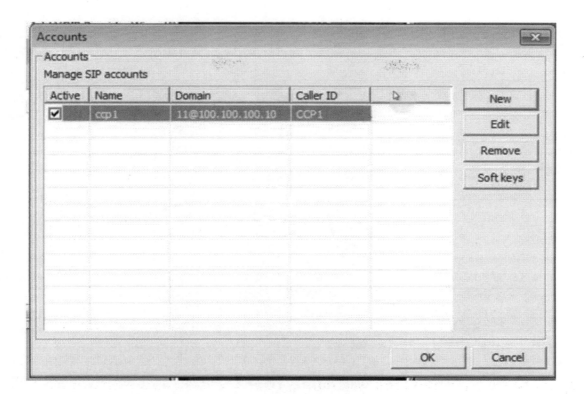

6) **After the information is inserted into the fields, click OK two times, the 3CX simulated phone will display "On Hook", display the present users name and the 3CXPhoneSystem server extension dot will turn "Green" indicating it is ready for a call.**

7) **Now just dial the other users' extension and wait for the phone to ring. If you have a camera connected, use the "Video Option". You can actually see the other callers face!!!!!**

Conclusion of the book:

You have reached the end of this text and I hope it has benefited you greatly. In the writing of this book, it was my desire to impart knowledge and methods which readers could use to increase their understanding of network technology. In addition, many sections are directly dedicated to both building network infrastructures as well as gaining network technology-related certifications. I hope you have benefited from my work and I wish you great success in all your adventures in network technology. Remember, ..."Knowledge First in All matters!!!!"

22255024R00104

Made in the USA
Columbia, SC
30 July 2018